# OLYMPIC HANDBALL

# OLYMPIC HANDBALL

**Lindsay Pennycook and Robin Sykes**

**Stanley Paul**

London Melbourne Sydney Auckland Johannesburg

Stanley Paul & Co. Ltd

An imprint of the Hutchinson Publishing Group

3 Fitzroy Square, London W1P 6JD

Hutchinson Group (Australia) Pty Ltd
30–32 Cremorne Street, Richmond South, Victoria 3121
PO Box 151, Broadway, New South Wales 2007

Hutchinson Group (NZ) Ltd
32–34 View Road, PO Box 40–086, Glenfield, Auckland 10

Hutchinson Group (SA) (Pty) Ltd
PO Box 337, Bergvlei 2012, South Africa

First published 1980

Set in Linotron Times

Printed in Great Britain by
Redwood Burn Limited       **46061794** ✕
Trowbridge & Esher

**British Library Cataloguing in Publication Data**

Sykes, Robin
    Olympic handball.
    1. Team handball
    I. Title   II. Pennycook, Lindsay
    796.31          GV1017.T4

    ISBN 0–09–141490–3
    ISBN 0–09–141491–1 Pbk

# Contents

Lindsay Pennycook, who wrote the major part of this book, gained an MA at Glasgow University and a Physical Education Diploma at Loughborough College. He is currently teaching in Dublin. He is one of Britain's longest-serving handball players, starting in 1967 and is currently national handball coach for Ireland. He has played in goal for Great Britain since 1972 and has taken part in Olympic qualifying and World Championship matches. He has travelled extensively in Europe, east and west, both as a player and a coach. He is also Irish 110 metre hurdle champion.

Robin Sykes is a former international athlete but is better known as an athletics coach. He holds a Diploma in Physiotherapy, a degree in Physical Education and currently lectures in Physical Education with Strathclyde Regional Council. He is the author of four books on sport and physical education.

**Acknowledgements**

In the production of this book, special thanks are due to Jim Leahy from the Art Department, Tallaght Community School, Co. Dublin for the work involved with the photography which features players from the Irish National and Irish Schools teams, pupils of Tallaght Community School and Scoil Aengus National School, Tallaght.

# Foreword

With the increasing popularity of Handball, the British Handball Association sees now the need for deeper development and welcomes this book, produced by two physical education teachers.

In the last ten years the game has grown from strength to strength in world terms as well as in the United Kingdom: so much so that the game has again been given full Olympic status for both men and women.

The Association is aware of the need to develop the game further especially in schools, and this text book will serve as a valuable aid to school teachers or physical educationalists wishing to introduce the game.

*Director of Coaching*
*British Handball Association*

# Preface

This book is the work of Lindsay Pennycook, an experienced International player and was produced with assistance from Robin Sykes who reviewed and edited the text, illustrations and presentation as well as contributing the two chapters on Training and Injuries, his specialist fields.

The book was written to fill an important vacuum in the development of handball in the British Isles. During the last decade, the sport of handball has been growing steadily in popularity and status, yet until now there has not been a comprehensive text to which teachers, coaches and players could refer for knowledge and guidance in all aspects of the sport from beginner to advanced level.

Teachers and PE undergraduates will find this book especially helpful as each chapter has been carefully prepared and structured to include teaching points, progressions, practices and material relevant to instruction. Practices have been graded throughout to cover all ranges of ability and special emphasis has been given to the methods and problems involved in the introduction and teaching of handball in schools, with particular reference to the teaching points, basic practices and techniques of the fundamental skills.

Coaches will be more concerned with the advanced parts of the early chapters and should make a detailed study of the principles and practices of individual and group attack and defence techniques, the operation of the systems of team offence and defence, the principles and phases of play, tactical moves, the training and technique of goalkeeping, the conditioning and training of players and the procedures for treating common injuries.

For players, this book offers for the first time an opportunity to read, analyse, evaluate and comprehend the essence of their chosen sport and consequently to emerge as more enlightened and talented.

Finally, we think it is the obligation of those who have benefitted from participation in sport in the form of personal enjoyment and recognition to put something of value back in return, and we hope this book will act as a catalyst towards the growth of this fascinating new sport not only in the British Isles but in other countries of the world.

## Key to symbols

|  |  |
|--------|---------|
| ○ | Goalkeeper |
| ○ | Defender |
| △ | Attacker |
| ⋮ | Handballs |
| C | Coach |
| R | Referee |
| – – – → | Pass |
| ← – – → | Pass back and forth |
| –∨– → | Bounce pass |
| ·········→ | Possible pass |
| ⟶ | Movement of player |
| ===⟹ | Movement of player with ball |
| ∿∿→ | Dribbling |
| ⟾ | Shot |
| ⟾ | Feinted shot |
| ⋯⋯⟾ | Possible shot |
| ==∧→⟾ | Jump shot |
| ∨→ | Feint or change of direction |
| ⟶⌐ | Block on player |
| ○← | Blocking the ball |
| –·–·–→ | Rolling the ball |
| ○• | Defender with ball |
| △• | Attacker with ball |

# 1 Introduction

Seven-a-side Olympic Handball is played in over 120 countries from as far afield as China, Zaire and East Germany to Brazil and the United States. It is one of the major sports of the world and was accorded Olympic status for men in Munich in 1972 and for women in Montreal in 1976.

Olympic Handball, also known as Team Handball, Continental Handball, European Handball and German Handball, is the second fastest ball team sport, combining the natural movements of running, jumping and throwing into a single yet dynamic game played by both men and women.

It is of no surprise to learn that handball is the major indoor sport in those countries where physical education is practised at its highest levels – Scandinavia and countries of Eastern Europe. Its growth and popularity is indicated by the increase in member nations of the International Handball Federation from eight in 1946 to the seventy-eight of today.

In the United Kingdom handball is rapidly gaining in status in schools, colleges, youth organizations, sports centres, the services and institutions of higher education etc.

## The game

As its name suggests, handball is a ball game played by the use of the hands. It is not to be confused with a popular sport in North America and Ireland also called handball but which is similar to squash. Olympic Handball is a team game played on a court indoors or outdoors on grass, tarmac, packed earth, clay or concrete. At each end of the court is a goal 2 metres high and 3 metres wide (photo 1). The two contesting teams each comprise seven players. During the game the ball is passed round team members from hand to hand, and a shot at goal is made when a player throws the ball

Photo 1

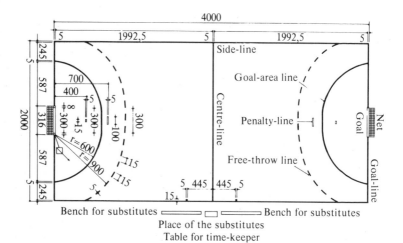

Figure 1

towards the opposition goal. When a team has possession they are classified as attackers and when possession is lost they become defenders.

All the action is focussed round the defending team's goal area which is marked in front in a 'D' shape 6 metres away from the goal line (figure 1). Only the goalkeeper plays in the goal area but court players can enter the area if they are in the air to shoot for goal. They can jump to enter the D (or propel themselves into it horizontally to gain additional power to their throw and also to get that much nearer to the actual target), but must release the ball before any part of their body touches the floor. It is an offence to violate the floor area of the D but not the air space. Defenders entering the goal area intentionally to prevent attackers from scoring are penalized by the award of a penalty. Defenders, therefore, form a defensive wall round the line to prevent attackers from shooting and scoring. Attackers pass the ball around quickly and use a variety of, often spectacular, shots to beat both the covering defence and the goalkeeper. For example they may shoot from a height by jumping up and firing over the defenders' hands; they may shoot low or to the side of defenders; and they can employ powerful angled shots from the wings.

Handball is a very fast game with comparatively few restrictions and players are constantly running, passing and shooting in a purposeful, aggressive manner. There is a need for regular substitution which can be made at any time without stoppages, from a team's pool of players (i.e. without having to call a 'time-out' as in basketball).

From a spectator's point of view handball is a fast, simple game which flows from end to end. It is a visually fascinating sport revolving round rapid, continuous ball movement which involves all the players. Energetic running on, and off, the ball and spectacular shooting results in goals or brings out fearless reflex saves from goalkeepers.

### Equipment

Handball is played indoors or outdoors on a court of regulation size approximately 120 by 60 feet (figure 1). Few schools have such large indoor areas but the game can be adapted quite easily to a smaller court. Until recently most school sports halls were constructed to accommodate the smaller basketball court and if this is the case handball could be played as a summer alternative outdoors. Indoor hockey, another fast-developing sport, is played on a handball court using the same line markings and where appropriate, therefore, both sports can be played in the same hall (goal dimensions in both games are also identical).

The goals are made of wood or aluminium. Often, in the early stages, teachers use make-shift goals borrowed from other games, for instance, soccer or outdoor hockey. If possible this should be avoided however, as it is imperative to use the regulation model from the outset. If goals cannot be obtained for any reason an improvised set may be produced by the woodwork department of the school or college. The most suitable design for such a set of home-produced goals is illustrated in photo 2. This portable set can be erected and dismantled with ease indoors or out; it is easily carried by hand and can be transported by minibus and stored neatly with little difficulty. Ideally schools and all sports centres should purchase a set of regulation goals for use not only in handball but also for indoor hockey and 5-a-side soccer (as played under continental rules).

Correct handballs (photo 3) should always be used, and these are now available in most sports shops. Schools are limited in many cases in the number of balls they can buy for various sports and the teacher can augment his supply by buying cheaper plastic soccer balls (size 3) which are excellent for initial practices. Basically there are three sizes of ball:

1  Mini ball for primary schools, boys under 14 and girls under 16
2  Youth or ladies' model for youths under 18 and women
3  Senior ball for men over 18

In the initial stages beginners and youngsters should use handballs with which they feel comfortable, irrespective of regulation size. Many learners in secondary schools, for example, have had no previous experience of handball and find the standard ball too large or too heavy to control. This can lead to frustration, boredom and ultimate rejection. The main objective with beginners is to get them to enjoy playing handball, and they should be encouraged to use whatever size of ball is best suited to them. Teachers should be careful not to over-inflate handballs as this not only tends to knock the balls out of shape but can increase the risk of bad finger injuries (see page 173).

The handball court with its line markings and names is described

Photo 2

Photo 3

in figure 1. In the early stages one should not worry overmuch about getting all the lines down before introducing the game; only the 6 metre line is essential – the remainder can be improvised.

Double-sided coloured jerseys or training bibs are useful in the early stages to distinguish teams. Cones can be used to mark training circuits, to act as defenders in practices or as targets at which to aim shots. Mats and jumping landing beds are excellent in teaching progressions for the fall shot (page 77).

## Qualities of handball

Many teachers quite often ignore new sports without due consideration to the value which a particular sport can add to the P E programme.

Handball is a particularly good game for youngsters because (as already mentioned) it is based on, and develops, the natural movements of running, jumping and throwing; it promotes physical fitness and trains the youthful body admirably. It is an athletic sport for young pupils who wish to express themselves in a fast, skilful game using their hands. It permits youngsters to release their aggressive energy constructively within the framework of relatively unrestricted rules. Aesthetically, handball is a sport which allows players to satisfy their natural, general activity drive through movement. For example, many young performers simply enjoy sport for sport's sake. It is accepted that movement can be rewarding in itself, can give pleasure to the performer *and* spectator as related to the visual awareness of shape and form. Briefly, there is a natural tendency towards symmetry, simplicity, closure and continuation of line – exactly the movements expressed in the play of a skilful, fast-moving handball team.

## Basic rules simplified

The complete laws of handball are published by the International Handball Federation. What follows is a simplified version explaining the basic rules and regulations and is sufficient for teachers and coaches at beginner and elementary level.

### Playing area

The playing area is 38 to 44 metres long and 18 to 22 metres wide. Line markings are as indicated in figure 1, namely:

goal line
goal area line
penalty line
free throw line
side line
centre line
substitution lines

## Ball

The ball consists of a rubber bladder encased in single-coloured leather, the men's model being 15 to 17 ounces in weight and 23 to 24 inches in circumference. Corresponding figures for ladies and youths are 11½ to 14 ounces and 21 to 22 inches.

## Goals

The goals are 2 metres high and 3 metres wide, of wood or synthetic material, painted on all sides in two colours (usually red and white stripes) with a securely attached net.

## Players

A team has twelve players of which two are goalkeepers, though only seven can play at a time (one, of course, being the goalkeeper). Goalkeepers are forbidden to play as court players but court players may, if the occasion arises, substitute for the keeper.

## Substitution

Players may enter as substitutes at any time and as often as required. A substitution cannot be made until the player leaving play has left the court between the substitution line and the centre line; the player going on does so within the same zone.

## Dress

All players dress similarly but the goalkeeper must be distinguishable. Players number from 1 to 12, number 1 being the first-choice keeper and number 12 the reserve custodian. Watches, rings, bracelets etc. are not permitted.

*Duration of the game*

The game consists of two halves each of 30 minutes, with a 10 minute interval. In tournaments the duration is two halves of 15 minutes each, with no interval. For ladies a game is two halves of 25 minutes with a 10 minute interval and in tournaments two halves of 10 minutes with no break. Time, as in soccer and rugby, may be added on for stoppages etc. and also to permit the outcome of a penalty or free throw. Teams change at half-time and in the case of a draw, where it has been agreed there must be a winner, they play two halves of 5 minutes extra with no interval.

*Start of the game*

The captain winning the toss has the choice of ends or throw-off. The throw-off must be taken within 3 seconds of the referee's whistle and both teams must be in their own half with the nearest opponent at least 3 metres from the ball. A goal cannot be scored direct from the throw-off.

*Scoring*

A goal is scored when the referee decides that the *whole* of the ball has crossed the goal line under the bar and between the two posts, provided the attacking team has not committed an offence. The ball is then put back into play as a consequence of the resultant throw-off.

*Goal area*

The goal area is that part of the court bounded by and inside the 6 metre goal area line (figure 1). Only the goalkeeper can play on the floor area in this zone. Any ball that enters and leaves the goal area without being touched by the goalkeeper remains in play. If a player deliberately plays the ball into his own area the referee will award the following:

  (i) a goal if the ball enters the net
 (ii) a penalty if the keeper stops the ball crossing his line
(iii) a 9 metre free throw for all other cases

Players entering the goal area are penalized as follows:

(i) a free throw if the attacker has possession of the ball
(ii) a free throw if an attacker without the ball gains a clear advantage
(iii) a penalty if the defender enters deliberately to gain a clear advantage

## Goalkeeper

The goalkeeper may use any part of his body to defend his goal. He has no restrictions in the goal area regarding steps or time but outside he is subject to the rules of court players. Entering or leaving his area he cannot *carry* the ball. (Penalty will result.)

## Playing the ball

A player is permitted to:

(i) stop, catch, throw, bounce or strike the ball in any manner and in any direction using hands (fists or open hands), arms, head, body, thighs and knees
(ii) hold the ball for a maximum of 3 seconds
(iii) place the ball from one hand to the other
(iv) pass the ball whilst sitting, kneeling or lying on the ground
(v) stop the ball with one or two hands then catch it without moving

A player is forbidden to:

(i) touch the ball more than once unless it touches the ground, another player, or the goal, is fumbled, or placed from one hand to the other
(ii) touch the ball intentionally with his leg (i.e. below the knee)
(iii) dive for the ball as it lies or rolls along the ground
(iv) deliberately play the ball over the side or goal line

NB: the goalkeeper is free from some of the above restrictions.

## Moving with the ball

A player may only take three steps while holding the ball. He may then stop, bounce the ball once with one hand and then take a further three steps. He may bounce the ball repeatedly with one hand while standing or running. Having caught the ball, however, he is allowed three steps and 3 seconds to hold it before passing or shooting. He may catch, bounce, catch the ball again when it has touched another player or the goal. There is no limit on the number of steps between bouncing and recatching the ball. A player can, if he wishes, roll the ball along the ground with one hand.

### Tackling the opposition

Players trying to dispossess the opposition are allowed to:

(i) use hands and arms to get hold of the ball
(ii) play the ball away from the opponent using the flat of the hand
(iii) obstruct with the body an opponent whether or not he is in possession of the ball

Players are forbidden to:

(i) snatch the ball violently using one or both hands or forcibly striking the ball out of an opponent's hands
(ii) hold or obstruct an opponent using hands, arms and legs
(iii) catch an opponent with one or both hands, handle him roughly by hitting, pushing, running into, jumping into, tripping or throwing himself before him
(iv) push or force an opponent into the goal area
(v) deliberately throw the ball at an opponent or thrust it towards him in a feint classed as dangerous

### Suspension of players

For ungentlemanly or dangerous conduct a player may be cautioned, suspended for 2 and 5 minute periods or suspended from the game. Substitutes cannot replace the suspended players except in the case of the goalkeeper when a court player must leave the play. Suspensions not completed in the first half are carried over.

### Goal throw

The goalkeeper throws the ball out from inside the goal area if the ball crossing the goal line was last played by an attacker or the keeper himself, or if the ball lands in the net direct from a throw-in, throw-off or goal throw. Opponents must be outside the 9 metre line and the ball is in play when it crosses the goal area line. The goalkeeper cannot score direct.

### Throw-in

This is awarded when the *whole* of the ball crosses the side line. The throw is taken from where the ball crossed the line by a member of the team in opposition to that of the player who last touched it.

### Corner throw

A corner throw is awarded when a defender last touched the ball before it crossed the goal line (keeper excepted). The throw is taken at the junction of the side line and the goal line (as in soccer) within 3 seconds of the referee's whistle, on the side that the ball went out of play. The player throwing must keep one foot on the floor and cannot play the ball until it touches another player or part of the goal. A goal can be scored direct and opponents must, again, be at least 3 metres from the ball.

### Free throw

A free throw is awarded for a variety of offences including:

   (i) illegally entering or leaving the court
  (ii) illegally playing the ball
 (iii) illegal defence, obstruction or tackling
  (iv) deliberately playing the ball out of play
   (v) stepping into the goal area
  (vi) minor infringements by the goalkeeper
 (vii) ungentlemanly conduct
(viii) infringements at set throws

The free throw may be taken immediately from the spot of the offence without waiting for the referee's whistle. For offences committed between the 6 and 9 metre lines the resultant free throw is taken from the nearest point outside the free throw line. No attackers can cross the 9 metre line until the throw is taken. Defenders, as always, must retreat 3 metres. If the throw is delayed then it must be executed within 3 seconds of the whistle. From the throw a goal can be scored direct. The taker must keep one foot on the floor and cannot touch the ball again until it has touched the goals or another player.

*Penalty throw*

The penalty is awarded for:

(i) dangerous play
(ii) destroying a clear chance of the opposition scoring a goal
(iii) intentionally entering the goal area for defensive purposes
(iv) intentionally playing the ball to one's own keeper
(v) the keeper carrying the ball in or out of his area
(vi) faulty substitution of the goalkeeper

Again one foot of the thrower must remain in contact with the floor during the execution of the throw which is taken from the 7 metre line (figure 1).

His throw must be taken within 3 seconds of the referee's whistle and the keeper may move in his area but not be closer than 3 metres to the thrower. Attackers stand outside the 9 metre line while defenders must be at least 3 metres from the ball.

*Referee's throw*

The game is restarted by a referee's throw if both teams commit an offence simultaneously, if a player accidentally falls on the ball delaying the game, or the game is unavoidably interrupted for any reason. The referee bounces the ball on the spot of the interruption or, if it is between the 6 and 9 metre lines, on the nearest point outside the 9 metre line. Players must stand at least 3 metres from the ball until it hits the ground.

*Officials*

Usually there are four officials to control a game of handball:

(i) two referees operating the dual system, responsible for enforcing the laws and for the smooth running of the game
(ii) a timekeeper for controlling the timing of the game, suspensions and entry of players
(iii) a scorer who keeps a record of the game (on many occasions this task is also undertaken by the timekeeper who may act in both a timekeeping and scoring capacity)

# 2 History, status and popularity

Handball, in common with other major world sports, has a long and eventful history. In Europe, before the emergence of the nation states, many isolated communities developed what would now be termed sports activities involving competition between individuals and groups to establish status and prestige, to gain peer acceptance, to attain reward and favour, for pleasure, or for the maintenance of physical fitness in preparation for possible attack from potential hostile invaders. As the major form of warfare at the time involved fighting with the use of the arms and the throwing of missiles such as spears and javelins, games and competitions developed involving the propulsion of objects by hand. A multitude of such games are recorded in the cultures of the diverse ethnic groupings in Europe; the Greeks played a game called Urania, the Romans played Harpastans and, later, Central Europeans in the middle ages developed *handballspiel*.

Thus, by the start of this century there existed a number of throwing games considered to be the forerunners of modern handball. These included Czeska Hasenka in Czechoslovakia, Handbold in Denmark and Korball and Raffbold in Germany. During the First World War an indoor version of 7-a-side handball began to take root; this was known as Torball and was later expanded in 1917 into an 11-a-side outdoor sport played on a soccer pitch with a soccer ball. Credit for this introduction goes to a German sports teacher called Heizer. This 11-a-side game increased in popularity in Germany and became known as handball. Soviet handball authorities claim handball (7-a-side) was developed in Kharkov by Edward Maly in 1909, only to be later eclipsed in the 1920s by the German 11-a-side version then dominant in Europe.

Similar games in other countries failed to develop in their own right and were gradually absorbed into the rules and codes of other sports. In Ireland for example the traditional throwing games contributed to, and were incorporated in, the formation of the rules of Gaelic football and still exist today in that sport in the form of the hand pass and in the hand method of scoring points and goals.

In 1926 the International Amateur Athletic Federation set up a committee to investigate the possibility of devising an internationally recognized code of rules. This Federation was, at that time, responsible for looking after minority sports. The rules were published two years later and in that same year, 1928, the International Amateur Handball Federation was established on the occasion of the Olympics in Amsterdam where a demonstration match was given. The Federation grew from eleven founder members to twenty-three by 1936 when outdoor handball was included in the Berlin Olympic Games. The host country won the gold medal and repeated this accomplishment in the first world championships two years later when ten countries entered.

During the Second World War handball stagnated, and in 1946 the old Federation was replaced by the present world body – the International Handball Federation (IHF). This step forward coincided with the change in popularity back from 11-a-side outdoor handball to the 'new' version of 7-a-side indoors. Eight countries were founder members of the IHF – Denmark, Sweden, Norway, Finland, France, Netherlands, Switzerland and Poland.

It was the change back to the 7-a-side version (which became popular both indoors and outdoors) that heralded the astonishing growth of the sport and which brought about the development of a fast, athletic and dynamic game based on spectacular movements of both players and ball concluding with precision shooting and fearless goalkeeping. The new sport became instantly attractive in a manner which the previous version had never been.

The first IHF indoor world championships were held in 1954 with Sweden emerging as the champions; three years later Czechoslovakia won the first ladies' championships. In 1956 the rules were revised to form the present laws and are still pretty much the same today. In 1972 handball was reintroduced into the Olympic Games and Yugoslavia took the gold medal; the status of handball as a major world sport was confirmed when the ladies' competition joined the men's in the Montreal Olympics four years later. In this particular Olympiad the USSR won both male and female competitions. The world championship is now a recognized event in the handball calendar and the sport is played in over 120 countries of the world.

The growth of handball since 1946 has been rapid; in the last decade North America, Asia and Africa, in particular, have taken enthusiastically to this game. Much of the credit for handball's growth in the newly emerging third world countries has been due to the influence of Eastern European coaches in those countries. The popularity of handball in Europe, especially in the eastern bloc, can be seen by studying the statistics of East Germany which many sports authorities hold as being the world's leading sports nation. This participants table (figure 2, from *Physical Culture in the GDR*) issued at the beginning of 1974 demonstrates handball's privileged place:

| | |
|---|---|
| badminton | 13,480 |
| basketball | 7,841 |
| *handball* | 180,031 |
| hockey | 5,616 |
| rugby | 765 |
| soccer | 487,570 |
| tennis | 30,635 |
| volleyball | 72,395 |

The Scandinavian countries pioneered the development of 7-a-side handball and were, for a time, the dominant playing nations. Now, however, the Eastern Europeans plus Denmark and West Germany are the world's leaders. Japan, the United States and Canada are making great strides to catch up and their recent international results have been encouraging. In North America, in many instances, handball has been rivalling basketball as the major indoor game. During the winter in Eastern Europe and Scandinavia the majority of outdoor ball sports cease due to the severity of the weather; sport moves indoor and this is where handball comes into its own. In western Europe, where the major ball games have a winter season, the development of handball as an alternative game is, at present anyway, less significant.

**Handball in the British Isles**

Handball in Great Britain is administered at all levels by the British Handball Association which was formed in 1967.

The first attempt to introduce handball into the British Isles was at Hull where a number of schools attempted to include the sport in their PE programme; this venture (at the start of the 1960s), however, failed to make any impact and eventually petered out. In 1965 Norwegian students at Heriot-Watt University wrote to fellow Scandinavians at other universities and colleges with a view to establishing handball clubs and competitions on a regular tournament basis. This proved successful and for the next few years tournaments were held at weekends at various venues. Taking part were student teams of Scandinavians from the Universities of Glasgow, Strathclyde, Heriot-Watt, Newcastle, Belfast (Queens) and from colleges in Sunderland and, later, Wolverhampton. The playing standard was high but only Glasgow made an effort to play home players. No attempt was made to spread the sport, run coaching courses, train referees or mould a national administrative structure. The emphasis remained on fun, enjoyment and socializing.

Two years later a group of physical-education teachers in the Liverpool area got together to introduce handball into their schools; these efforts at last proved positive and from this base on Merseyside senior clubs were created and the British Handball Association formed. The game soon spread to the north east, midlands and south east where strong clubs emerged to challenge the Merseyside and student teams already mentioned.

In 1968 the British Handball Association was granted full membership of the IHF. The national men's team played in the 1972 and 1976 Olympic qualifying tournaments and later in the World Championship Group C matches in Portugal, giving an extremely competent account of themselves. The national ladies' team play regularly on the continent and the national men's club champions compete each year in the European Club Championships. There are regular home internationals for men and ladies involving the home countries.

Handball in Scotland is administered by the Scottish Handball Association a body founded in 1972 with considerable autonomy.

Handball in Republic of Ireland and in Northern Ireland is administered by the Irish Olympic Handball Association formed in 1975. Ireland was granted provisional membership of the IHF in 1978.

# 3 Introductory school games and simple activities

The introduction and teaching of any new sport to youngsters must be related to their level of maturity; this particular chapter is geared towards the 10 to 15 year olds i.e. those in the late stages of primary school and the first three years of secondary.

In the actual game the teacher should ensure the maximum amount of play in a natural, adventuresome and enjoyable manner. Continuity and spontaneity can be maintained and encouraged by modifying the rules in the early stages. The more active and involved the beginner is the greater are the chances of skill acquisition and, just as important, his appetite for the game being whetted. At first learners should be allowed to play without stress on any particular skill or specialization in court positions and should progress through a diversity of auxiliary activities as well as being allowed to experience situations which will produce sufficient exercise value. Coaching should be minimal but games should be stopped periodically to illustrate, for example, a better move, shot or pass, etc. If a keeper dives to save as in soccer, play should be halted to demonstrate the proper handball technique involving the use of the legs to stop low shots (see pages 96 and 100).

With younger age groups especially, there may be no real necessity to work through a planned scheme of progressions; employing a wide range of fun activities using basic handball movements and skills could be, perhaps, more productive. There are at least four games through which the teacher can introduce an appreciation of handball concepts. Without such a carefully graded initial development, learners would play handball as if it were soccer.

## Handball concepts for beginners

There are a number of concepts which *must* be appreciated by learners if they are to proceed with a positive approach to the game;

these concepts are related to the basic rules on pages 16–22 and to the skills illustrated on pages 40–46, i.e.:

(i) catching in two hands and passing in one (in previous team sports youngsters may well have been instilled with the two-handed form of passing as in rugby, basketball, soccer throw-in, etc.)

(ii) shooting for goal with a smaller and lighter ball than they may hitherto have experienced

(iii) running with and without the ball – handball has a high content of running combined with evasive dodging and chasing and is played at a faster pace than most sports

(iv) understanding the privileged position of the goalkeeper in his own zone; learners often find it difficult to accept and understand that the keeper should have an area exclusively to himself

(v) Attack–defence relationship – this is the most difficult concept for young players to grasp. To stand in defence round the 6 metre line whilst attackers are playing the ball around virtually unopposed is an alien concept in Britain where the tendency is to go and chase after the ball, as in soccer

(vi) high scoring rate – goals in handball occur with much greater frequency than in most games and youngsters should not be discouraged if their team falls a few goals behind – games can, and often do, change quite radically

(vii) physical contact – handball allows physical contact to about the same degree as soccer and considerably more than in basketball

*Introductory school games*

Four games best incorporate the concepts described above:

(i) headball
(ii) benchball
(iii) deadball
(iv) pin handball

All these games should be played competitively with the emphasis on fun, enjoyment and total participation. All can be played with one ball and the minimum of equipment either indoors or outdoors on any size of playing area. If the numbers involved are large,

Photo 4

ensure that teams are constantly changed over to maintain continuity of play with *all* youngsters getting equal play opportunity.

## Headball

Headball, as the name implies, involves the scoring of goals using only the head (photo 4) and, as such, is soccer-related. Two teams face each other with a goal at each end of the court; the dimension of the goal can vary, but 5 metres wide and 2½ metres high would suffice. They are roughly the same shape as soccer goals and can be taped or painted on the wall or indicated by the use of two badminton stands as it is visually simple for the teacher to judge the height of the goals when a scoring effort goes high. A player is permitted three steps, bounce and pass (or a further three steps after the bounce) to a team-mate who can score by heading the pass for goal from anywhere on the court or pitch. The keeper, as in handball, is the only player allowed to use his feet (for saving purposes, of course, not for propulsion of the ball). Players dispossess the opposition by intercepting their passes, gathering loose balls (misplaced passes, attempts at goal, etc.) or getting the ball from opponents who are dribbling. A certain amount of physical contact is allowed and the players are subsequently introduced to, and will accept, a number of handball features:

  (i)   use of hands, not feet, to move the ball around
 (ii)   running three steps with the ball, then bounce or pass
(iii)   fast-flowing end to end play with quick throws and breaks absolutely essential
(iv)   a high number of goals
  (v)   an acceptable amount of body contact
(vi)   an understanding that only the goalkeeper may use his feet

For this particular game a volleyball or size 5 plastic soccer ball is best; an actual handball itself tends to be too small.


*Benchball*

This game is suitable for girls as well as boys. Two teams (each with a keeper) play, as in headball, but instead of goals two benches are placed at the end of the sports hall with a keeper standing on each (photo 5). (NB each team's keeper is in front of the team, not behind as usual, and is standing on the bench defended by the opposition.) He may move along the bench but is not allowed to come off nor can a court player step on to the bench. In this game a handball can be used and is passed, by hand, round the members of the team. A goal is scored when a player throws the ball to his own goalkeeper (standing on the opposition's bench, remember) who must catch the ball cleanly in two hands whilst remaining balanced on the bench. A player may take the standard three steps, bounce, pass or shoot and when one team has possession the other retreats to form a defensive wall round the bench. The ball cannot be fisted or played by the feet. Benchball introduces:

  (i)   handpassing as in handball
 (ii)   shooting for goal with one hand
(iii)   running three steps, bounce, pass or shoot
(iv)   shooting over or through a defensive set-up
  (v)   attack–defence relationship – when one team attacks the other forms a defensive wall round the goalkeeper

Photo 5

(vi)  a fast-flowing high-scoring game
(vii)  speed *off* the ball – this is vital

*Deadball*

Unlike the previous games this is not a team contest but contains a competitive element on an individual basis. One boy is selected from the class and makes himself distinguishable from the others (by wearing training bib, taking off his vest etc.). The rest of the class scatter round the gym or games hall and are then chased by this boy who tries to hit them with the ball below shoulder height (photo 6). When one is hit he joins forces with the thrower and these two chase the remainder. From then on each player who is hit joins the chasers but now the three step rule comes into operation when the thrower can (after his three strides) either pass to another chaser or shoot. Players being chased may defend themselves with their fists without this being classed as a hit against them. The game continues until only one player (the winner) is left. Deadball helps to introduce:

   (i) powerful and accurate shooting
  (ii) players passing around as a handball *team*, taking three steps, bounce, pass/shoot
 (iii) players running constantly watching the movement of ball and opposition simultaneously
 (iv) introduces swerves, turns, dodges and, a key factor in the game – *change of pace and direction*
  (v) instils the need for patient build-up of play
 (vi) gives practice in passing and shooting whilst moving at speed
(vii) demonstrates the value of passing to a player who is in a better position than oneself

Photo 6

To make deadball more realistic and adventuresome each player may be allowed to shoot only from the jumping position or with a bounce, prior to the introduction of correct shooting techniques (pages 70–93). In addition, gymnastic equipment can be positioned round the gym (e.g. benches, sections of the box, crash landing mats etc.) behind which the players can hide.

*Pin handball*

A cone or similar object is positioned at either end of the gym or games hall inside a chalked semi-circle or even for convenience a basketball "key". No one is allowed inside this zone. Two teams play against each other, passing the ball around and scoring when they hit the opposition's cone (photo 7) . To prevent a goal the defensive team form a wall round the semi-circle and attempt to block shots going in; defending players entering the zone are penalized by a penalty throw taken from about 7 metres distant. The ball is passed and shot as in previous games. Thus, earlier concepts are re-

Photo 7

inforced especially that of a keeper's zone into which defensive intrusion is forbidden and is punishable by a penalty throw.

A class exposed to the four games mentioned above will be constantly picking up basic handball skills, ideas, movements and tactics, in other words, getting the *feel* of the game so that the introduction of handball itself requires only refinement and adjustment to existing expertise.

**Handball – the game situation at beginner level**

Having exposed the class to the introductory, transitional games, the teacher can modify the actual game of handball by introducing temporary rules to maintain continuity. In order to ensure the correct balance between attack and defence a penalty should be awarded for the following three offences:

  (i) a defender entering the goal area to gain advantage
 (ii) defenders crossing their own 9 metre line as the attackers are playing the ball around – this prevents the defenders from running all over the court as in soccer, thereby spoiling the game
(iii) when a team have lost possession and they fail to get back to their own 6 metre line within 5 seconds

The game should be stopped from time to time to demonstrate and introduce skills and teaching points. Players should be encouraged to jump into the 'D' to shoot from an early stage. All players rotate round positions including goalkeeper and the lesson should be conducted on the whole–part–whole basis with selected skill practices as appropriate.

**Minor activities**

A number of simple handball-related activities are useful for the younger age groups from an enjoyment viewpoint.

An adaptation of the old favourite – 'dodge ball' (figure 3). A players pass the ball round and across to hit B players. When hit, B players sit down and the remainder must dodge round to avoid being hit till the last B player is eliminated.

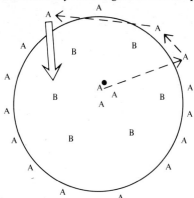

Figure 3

A number of boxes and benches are placed round the gym (figure 4). Two teams of equal numbers are selected; players A try to hit players B and vice versa. When a player is hit he sits down and so on until one team is completely eliminated.

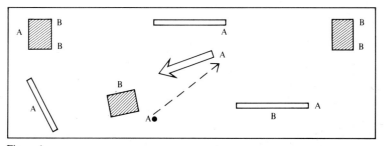

Figure 4

Players throw the ball over a net (figure 5 – vary the height of the net as for tennis, volleyball, etc.) from both running and jumping positions. Throwers must keep the ball in the court area. If the opposition catch the ball cleanly they gain a point – conversely if they drop the ball or fail to catch cleanly they lose a point.

Figure 5

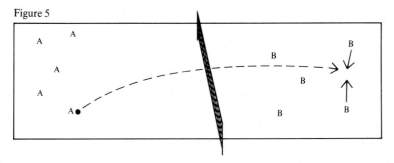

Players from team A stand on one bench and B players on the other (figure 6). Players A shoot to hit those on Bs' bench and vice versa. When hit, a player joins shooters at the side.

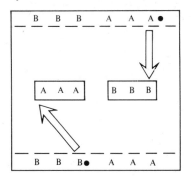

Figure 6

A cone is situated in a circle (figure 7). With team A defending, team B pass the ball around and have to hit the cone three times in succession. If they fail to do so the teams switch.

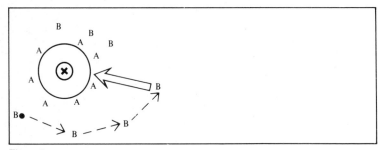

Figure 7

Players B guard a cone in the middle of a big circle (figure 8); A players pass around and shoot to hit cone. After five scores two A players replace the B members.

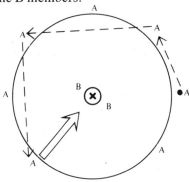

Figure 8

# 4 Basic skills

**Skills**

A good handball player requires:

  (i)  a high degree of technical skill
 (ii)  an equally high degree of physical fitness
(iii)  a thorough knowledge and understanding of tactics
(iv)  the correct mental approach

In handball the degree of technical skill is the most important and the skills of a handball player are manifest in a series of organized, co-ordinated activities involving the use of sensory and motor mechanisms. To enable a skill to be acquired the individual must have the inherent potential to learn such behaviour and have a suitable environment at his disposal. Skill acquisition requires players to be under the guidance of knowledgeable coaches experienced in nursing their charges through this complex yet apparently simple process.

There are seven basic handball skills:

  (i)  running
 (ii)  jumping
(iii)  throwing (passing and shooting)
(iv)  catching
 (v)  blocking and gaining possession
(vi)  dribbling
(vii)  body movements of turning, twisting, faking and swerving

*Running*

Owing to the nature of the sport, with its free and unrestricted rules, running assumes more importance in handball than in most sports. Practices should include running forwards, backwards and sideways. Players must be able to accelerate rapidly from a standing start, maintain fast, constant bursts of speed and change pace and direction as required.

## Jumping

Jumping is a vital skill. In attack, for example, it is often necessary for a player to jump before he shoots over the defence. Defensively it is equally important for players round the 6 metre line to be able to jump high enough to block the jump shot, especially the central defenders covering the best shooting angles. Thus, players need to pay particular attention to leg strengthening exercises which should be practised on a regular basis.

## Throwing

Throwing, in the form of passing and shooting, is absolutely fundamental. Technique, accuracy and timing can only be learned in practices on passing and catching (pages 60–69) and on shooting (pages 83–93).

## Catching

Catching is necessary for individual control, the maintenance of team possession, and for the variety of options which a secure catch offers, e.g. pass, dribble or shot, all of which increase in effectiveness if the ball is correctly caught at speed during movement.

## Blocking and gaining possession

The blocking of shots is an individual defensive skill, which is described on pages 133–4. Blocking, and at the same time acquiring the ball, has a double benefit for a team in that it not only gains them possession but it enables constructive attacking moves to be set up whether it be the fast break (page 115) or a recognized system of attack (pages 151–60).

## Dribbling

Dribbling permits a player to travel with the ball; it slows down movement, however, and should not be encouraged except in cer-

Photo 8          Photo 9

tain specific situations such as the fast break. Effective dribbling requires close control with the player pushing the ball to and from the floor with his fingers spread well apart (photos 8 and 9). When moving at speed the player must push the ball sufficiently well ahead and most learners find this awkward in the initial stages. Dribbling practices can help to bring added interest to training sessions (pages 44–45).

*Body movements*

The skills of turning, twisting, faking and swerving are rarely evident in beginners and only develop when the fundamental skills of passing, catching and shooting have been acquired and mastered. They are particularly effective as individual attacking skills and are described in greater depth on pages 151–57. In brief, they require close ball control, confidence, anticipation and the element of surprise.

With beginners the teacher or coach should concentrate on running, jumping, catching, passing and shooting with dribbling practices thrown in for variety. Simple skill circuits are effective especially if run on a competitive basis. For advanced players the skills must be analysed and learned in accordance with proven scientific and biomechanical principles and players should be advised to read about training methods and schedules from other sports which involve the development of related skills and movements, e.g. for jump shooters, high-jump training methods from track and field; for goalkeepers, mobility work and muscle control from ballet and gymnastic training; for wingers, twists, turns, and other body movements also through gymnastics.

### Simple group practices for basic beginner skills

*Running practices*

These involve a series of running and relay competitions in either the gym or the games hall and can include, for example, the following activities:

(i) simple down and back relay (figure 9): each member of competing teams sprints to the wall and back

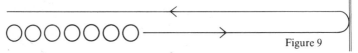

Figure 9

(ii) bench relay (figure 10): each player hurdles the bench en route to the wall, returns to touch the bench, up to the wall again and, finally, a hurdling sprint again back to his next runner

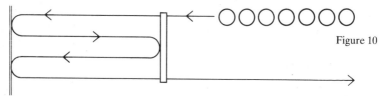

Figure 10

(iii) zigzag relay (figure 11): each player runs between the cones/markers to the wall and back

Figure 11

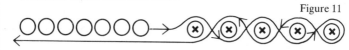

(iv) grid iron relay (figure 12): out to B, back to A, out to C, back
to A, out to D, back to A, etc.

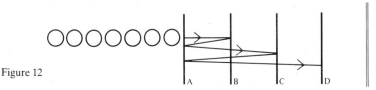

Figure 12

Relay runs round a circuit marked by cones (figure 13).

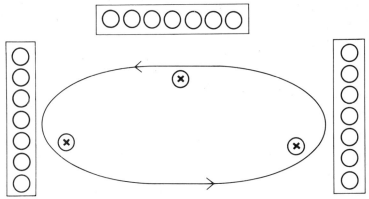

Figure 13

  (i) each player runs two consecutive laps
 (ii) each player runs one lap backwards
(iii) each player runs one lap sidestepping (heels clicking together
in mid-air)
(iv) each player hops one lap
 (v) each player runs one lap running a full circle round each cone
(vi) each player runs one lap in rotation, the team covering the
most laps after, say, 3 minutes being the winners
(vii) pursuit run: teams run together until one is lapped by the
other

In single file the players complete the running circuit (figure 14) as
follows:

A–B  sprint between the 6 and 9 metre lines in zigzag fashion touching the lines with the feet and holding the hands high as in the
defensive position described on page 128
B–C  sprint as in fast break (page 115)

C–D  sideways round the 6 metre line to simulate lateral movement
      of defence (feet don't cross)
D–A  relaxed jog with dropped arms

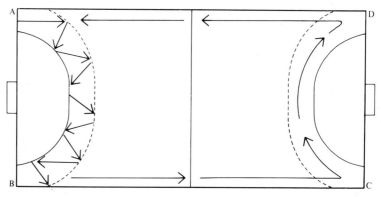

Figure 14

*Simple jumping practices*

*Figure 15*: coach throws the ball between two lines of players (as in
rugby line-out). Every attempt should be made to take the ball
cleanly.

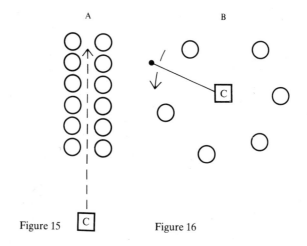

Figure 15                    Figure 16

*Figure 16*: the players form a circle with the coach in the middle; he
then swings a rope with a shoe/boot/rubber ring etc., on the end of it
whilst the players must jump up to avoid the rope.

*Figure 17*: players line up and run to jump up and head a towel or jersey suspended from a beam. Alternatively a basketball ring and net may be used or any other improvisation.

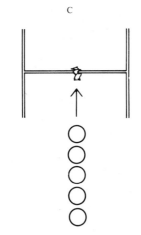

C

Figure 17

*Simple passing and catching practices*

*Figure 18*: long throws the length of the hall.

Figure 18

*Figure 19*: players passing and catching while moving at varying paces.

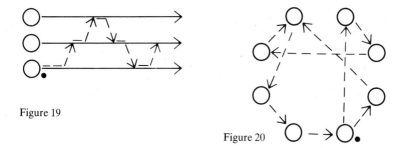

Figure 19

Figure 20

*Figure 20*: passing round and across a circle.

*Simple shooting practices* (figure 21)

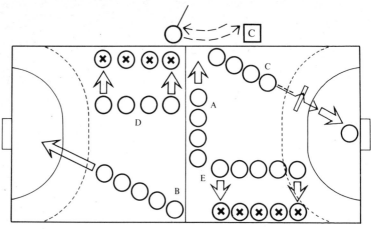

Figure 21

A.  players shoot at a weight suspended from a rope which the coach keeps swinging like a pendulum
B.  players shoot to hit the uprights or crossbar
C.  players jump over bench to shoot past keeper
D.  players kneel on the floor and fall forward to shoot at cones
E.  players bounce-shoot to knock over cones

*Dribbling practices* (all grades of ability)

*Figure 22*: A dribbles round the markers, passes to B and joins the end of B's line. B dribbles, passes to C then joins the end of his line, the whole sequence being kept going continuously as required. This can be made competitive by the addition of a rival team.

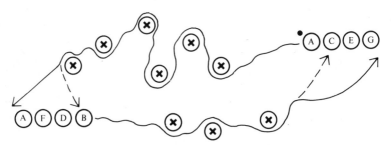

Figure 22

*Figure 23*: A dribbles, passes to B, receives pass back, dribbles, passes to C, receives pass back, dribbles and passes to D then joins the end of D's line. D repeats in opposite direction.

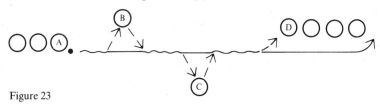

Figure 23

*Figure 24*: A dribbles up the line of markers; when he crosses the finishing line he turns quickly and passes back to B who does the same before returning to C, etc. A good competitive type of relay between teams – first team with all players over the finishing line are the winners.

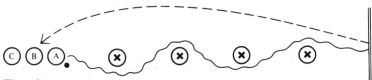

Figure 24

*Figure 25*: A passes to B, receives the return pass at speed and dribbles as fast as possible up court to the finishing line. B, having given the pass, sprints off after him trying to dispossess before A reaches the finishing line.

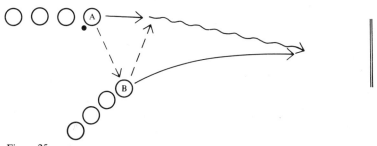

Figure 25

*A simple circuit involving all the basic skills* (figure 26)

Position a goalkeeper in one of the goals and divide the class or players into six groups of four as follows:

Group 1   ABCD   *sprinting*   one length of the court in turn
Group 2   EFGH   *dribbling*   one length of the court in turn
Group 3   JKLM   *passing*   round a square marked by mats or cones
Group 4   NOPQ   *jumping*   players squat-jump in turn from the 9 metre line to touch the wall and then run back
Group 5   RSTV   *sideways/backwards running*   each player, in turn, runs to the wall sideways, returning by running backwards
Group 6   WXYZ   *shooting*   each player jumps over a bench on the 9 metre line and attempts to score past the goalkeeper with a jump shot. Players retrieve their own ball

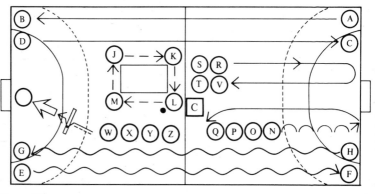

Figure 26

The coach stands in the middle of the court and blows his whistle for the activities to commence. Each activity is worked at for 2 minutes (or any other period of time which might be considered appropriate) and then scores are recorded on a blackboard. After a 30 second rest groups move round in rotation to the next activity and so on until all have been completed. The scores are then totalled up on a descending scale, e.g. team with the most number of goals etc. gets 6 points, second 5, third 4 and so on. This is completed for all the activities and the team with the highest number of points from the six wins. The board is marked and scored as in figure 27:

Figure 27: Activities

| Groups | Sprinting No. | Pts | Dribbling No. | Pts | Jumping No. | Pts | Passing No. | Pts | Running No. | Pts | Shooting No. | Pts | Total | Place |
|---|---|---|---|---|---|---|---|---|---|---|---|---|---|---|
| 1 | 28 | 4 | 24 | 3 | 56 | 5 | 61 | 5 | 41 | 5 | 21 | 6 | 28 | 1st |
| 2 | 26 | 2 | 23 | 2 | 52 | 4 | 63 | 6 | 40 | 4 | 16 | 5 | 23 | 2nd |
| 3 | 30 | 5 | 18 | 1 | 57 | 6 | 60 | 4 | 39 | 3 | 15 | 4 | 23 | 2nd |
| 4 | 27 | 3 | 25 | 4 | 48 | 1 | 54 | 2 | 37 | 2 | 8 | 1 | 13 | 6th |
| 5 | 25 | 1 | 27 | 5 | 49 | 2 | 52 | 1 | 43 | 6 | 11 | 3 | 18 | 5th |
| 6 | 32 | 6 | 28 | 6 | 51 | 3 | 57 | 3 | 35 | 1 | 10 | 2 | 21 | 4th |

# 5 Principles and practice of passing and catching

Handball is basically a simple game in which the aim is to win by scoring goals. To achieve this a team must gain and retain possession, by skilful passing, intelligent positioning, movement and leadership. For both passing and catching the correct techniques and skills must be acquired and practised regularly. Too often, at all levels of handball, promising, constructive tactical moves and plays break down through poor, unimaginative or careless passes.

The best passers in handball are distinguished by their ability to combine to a high degree at least four principles of passing:

(i) *accuracy* – the pass being directed to the *precise* required destination

(ii) *timing* – the instinct to know the *exact* moment the ball should be released

(iii) *angles* – knowing where to pass the ball to allow the maximum return in terms of *positive* play

(iv) *weighting* – the ability to judge the feel of the ball and to determine how *hard* to pass the ball in given situations according to distance and positioning of colleagues

In the higher levels of handball there is obviously more to passing than the correct application of the technical skills and the top-class passers in international handball display, to varying degrees, imagination, opportunism, inventiveness, instinct and, most of all, *simplicity*. At all times the *receiver*, of course, must want the ball, look for it, desire to control it and make *full* use of it.

## Catching

The ability to catch a ball securely is a fundamental handball skill. The basic principle in the handling of the ball is to cushion or check its speed, secure possession and control it immediately. Both hands are used to catch the ball and they should remain relaxed.

*Fundamental principles and teaching points*

  (i)  eyes focussed on the moving ball

 (ii)  arms held in the outstretched position with the fingers relaxed and spread out pointing in the direction of the in-
coming ball (photo 10)

Photo 10

(iii)  the arms and fingers begin to flex as the ball approaches,
cushioning the speed of the ball. The fingers act as shock
absorbers (photos 11 and 12)

Photo 11                           Photo 12

(iv) the ball is pulled in close to the chest into a very secure and protective position (photo 11)

(v) it is then quickly transferred into a good position for distribution in the form of pass, dribble, shot or other movement

(vi) throughout these movements the receiver must be in the correct, balanced position, ideally moving slightly towards the ball, legs flexed, one foot ahead of the other, weight distributed forwards (photo 12)

(vii) passes received above waist height are caught with the hands spread out, fingers flexed pointing upwards with the thumbs touching to form a 'W' shape (figure 28). Below waist height the hands are inverted and touch only with contact of the little fingers. To catch a very low ball securely it is often necessary to stretch one foot out in front of the other, sinking very low with the leading leg flexed and the knee of the extended rear leg almost touching the floor; the hands remain inverted (photo 13)

Figure 28

Photo 13

(viii)   players must be able to take passes which stray high, low or to the side both from stationary or moving positions, often during twisting and turning movements at speed

These general principles are basic to both learners and advanced players. They should be practised constantly during training sessions for it is catching and passing which deteriorates first when a team finds itself under stress in a match situation. When introducing catching to beginners teachers should emphasize and reinforce the above teaching points. One of the most difficult principles for learners to appreciate is the value and effectiveness of cushioning the ball as it reaches the outstretched arms (this is similar to the soccer player receiving a hard pass often from short range which he must 'kill' by controlling with the limp lower leg). Apart from reducing the incidence of finger injuries it allows for greater security of control and, more important, maintains the team's possession of the ball. To emphasize this point try hanging a jersey over the crossbar and throw the ball at the jersey; even a particularly fierce pass or shot will fall down on to the floor because of the natural cushioning and 'absorbing' effect of the jersey.

**Passing**

The shoulder pass is the simplest, most natural and most effective method of passing the ball from one player to another. When the ball is held in the correct position players can decide to pass or shoot (shoulder shot) or continue forward in a comfortable, relaxed and controlled manner with possibilities of individual attack using twists, turns, feints accompanied by changes in direction and pace (possibilities more fully described in chapter 10). The shoulder pass is by far the most popular pass and is the medium used to describe best the principles and teaching points for passing.

*Principles and Teaching Points* (photos 14 and 15 and figure 29)

   (i)   ball rests on the palm of the passing hand
  (ii)   the passing arm is held high and back
 (iii)   the arm is bent at the elbow
 (iv)   the leading leg is forward and flexed
  (v)   the foot of the leading leg points forward in the direction of the pass while the foot of the rear leg points slightly to the side

Photo 14

Figure 29

Photo 15

Figure 30

(vi) the non-throwing arm is held across the chest and the shoulder is often slightly lowered as the pass is executed
(vii) as the throw is made the player's weight moves forward into a follow-through action
(viii) the execution of the throw is led by the elbow, followed by the forearm and, finally, the wrist flick
(ix) this final wrist flick is important for adding both control and direction to powerful, accurate passes (figure 30)

*Shoulder pass*

This pass must be mastered from both stationary and moving (sometimes at top speed) positions. The running shoulder pass is used when teaching beginners how to pass while in motion but should soon be dropped as an isolated passing practice. Handball passing movements should all be executed by players constantly on the move. Beginners using the running shoulder pass tend to pass the ball with too much force forgetting that the ball is already moving forwards by the very fact that they themselves are in motion. Much of the power, therefore, for the running pass comes only from the forearm and wrist.

## Cross-body pass

This pass is used when a team is playing the ball across the court from right to left (assuming all the players are right handed – photo 16). Instead of catching the ball, turning the trunk to face, and shoulder passing to the next player, a passer will, on securing the ball in the hands, whip a pass across the body and over to a team-mate. With the ball being caught between the waist and head this pass allows a player to pass without upsetting his forward or backward momentum. It is particularly effective when used by the big 9 metre shooters driving in on the defence and quickly releasing the pass to the next player on the left. Players receiving this pass while driving for goal have possibilities of beating a defender in a one-against-one situation (page 155) or releasing a similar pass to the nearest player in a lightning movement to create extra time and space. The pass is, therefore, very effective during phases of fast, direct, attack by the big shooters from the attacking back division.

## Side wrist pass

This pass is used when a team is playing the ball across the court from left to right. The reasons for this quick, short pass are the same as for the cross-body pass – speed of movement to create additional time and shooting space. On catching the ball the player moves it in both hands to around waist height. The right forearm is flexed and rotated so that the hand comes over to the left side of the ball (photo 17); from there it is propelled by a very strong wrist flick out to the player's right or vice versa for a left hander (photo 18). The side wrist pass is extremely effective over short distances and is easily mastered by players with a wide hand span; those with small hands or beginners with weak wrist and finger muscles may find this pass difficult unless the ball (as is usual) has been coated with a sticky substance to improve the players' grip.

## Bounce pass

This pass (together with the remaining ones) is only used in certain situations and can, therefore, be considered as a secondary pass.

The bounce pass (photo 19) is employed under some circumstances by intelligent players in given situations. The pass is not governed by any particular rule but it takes longer to reach its desti-

Photo 16

Photo 17

Photo 18

Photo 19

nation than the shoulder pass and is, consequently, vulnerable to interception. Novices should be discouraged from using this pass in the game situation but, for reasons explained later, it is an important practice when teaching the shoulder pass.

*Jump pass*

When a player leaps into the air to jump shoot he sometimes realises, within a split second, that his chances of scoring have quite suddenly deteriorated. So, instead of shooting, and running the risk of losing possession for his team, he would release the ball at some stage of the jump, passing it to a team-mate. The jump pass is often used as an intentional pass in the form of a jump 'feed' through to a line player who has moved into space behind a defender drawn out to block the jump shot on the 9 metre line.

Photo 20

## Chest pass

This two-handed pass, derived from basketball, is of limited value and is used only over very short distances as a fast pass at chest height. During the execution of the pass the ball is held close to the chest with the arms flexed and elbows forward. The propulsion for the ball comes from the action of the thumbs and fingers which push the ball out vigorously (photo 20). The chest pass is effective either when used by two players sprinting up the court in close proximity following, for example, an interception, or in the making of a fast break.

## Underhand pass

The underhand pass is used in specific situations by experienced players and is of value when the ball is fed through to a line player as it can travel under the arms of the defenders. The ball is caught in two hands and taken behind the hip in the throwing hand then brought forward with a straight arm to be pushed off from behind and underneath.

### Drop pass

This pass is used when a shooter advances in towards the 9 metre line to shoot for goal. The player goes through the motions of shooting but at the last moment, with the defence committed, he drops the ball out of his hand at its furthest extremity (figure 31). As the

Figure 31

ball is passed backwards to a team-mate the passer *must* have signalled previously or have a good *understanding* with his fellow players. This drop pass requires precise timing and accuracy and is not recommended for beginners.

### Concealed passes

It should, perhaps, be mentioned here that there are a number of concealed passes – behind the back (photo 21), behind the head (photo 22), two-hand overhead, etc. – but these may only serve to confuse the reader. It is best to master those described above leaving these specific concealed passes to those who have reached a high playing standard and who know from experience and training when to play these often unorthodox passes, effective as they may sometimes be, in, for example, a two-against-one attack.

Photo 21

Photo 22

*Common faults in beginners*

   (i)  holding the ball using the fingers instead of resting the ball in the palm of the passing hand

  (ii)  the shooting arm held too low and not as far back as possible – this can sometimes be the result of a lack of shoulder mobility

 (iii)  no final flick from the wrist

 (iv)  wrong leg forward when passing

  (v)  passing the ball too high and too hard

 (vi)  disruption of natural stride pattern when shoulder passing whilst on the move

 (vii)  ball slipping out of the hand when trying the side wrist pass

(viii)  those with basketball experience bounce the ball unnecessarily often and chest pass to extreme

 (ix)  those with netball experience stop and look all around for support then, possibly, lob the passes

### Holding the ball

Following a catch a player may hold the ball for the permitted 3 seconds before bouncing it, passing it, or shooting for goal. During this short time he has full control over the ball which is held at chest height to allow the maximum number of options. If the ball is held in one hand away from the chest then it is vulnerable to a loss of possession to an opponent. When the ball is at chest height it is held firmly by the fingers which are spread out and pointing forwards (photo 23). This *firm grip* on the ball is particularly important for line players who, on receiving a pass, twist and turn in an attempt to find an opportunity for a fall or dive shot. Holding the ball in one hand, however, allows a player to drive in on goal and to beat an opponent in a one-against-one situation. Control of a ball held in one hand during movement requires strong forearm muscles, fingers and wrists, which can be strengthened through exercises (pages 169–171). Generally the holding of the ball should be at chest height in two hands and should be as brief as possible as it breaks the continuity of passing movements, allowing defenders time to think and to counter carefully planned attacking tactics.

### Passing and catching practices for beginners

For beginners and improvers the teacher and coach should ensure there is one ball per player especially in the initial stages. The use of

Photo 23

a plastic soccer ball (size 3) was mentioned in chapter 1 and the practices have been organized to suit the needs of the teacher with one ball per player and later for those with, say, four balls per class.

British schoolchildren are generally poor passers of a handball, partly due to lack of exposure to throwing activities and partly because most of the ball games to which they have been introduced involve handling bigger, heavier balls (basketball, rugby, soccer). Catching, holding and passing a small light ball is a strange and novel sensation for most youngsters; because of this a great deal of practice is required to develop the correct basic technique.

## Sitting position

The best method for developing the correct technique is from the seated position, legs extended out in front, the students facing each other or a wall at a distance of about 2 metres.

The passing arm is raised with the elbow flexed and held back as far as possible. The ball rests in the palm of the hand and is thrown forward against the wall using forearm, fingers and wrist (photo 24). Power and technique is improved by increasing the distance from the wall. This seated position maintains a disciplined approach if thirty beginners are standing throwing handballs for the first time and avoids chaos.

To introduce and emphasize the final flick of the wrist each player holds the forearm of the passing arm with his other hand while he passes (photo 25).

This helps to develop the power of the wrist.

### *Standing and running positions*

1 *One player per ball*
 (i) each player stands opposite a wall about 3 metres distant, catching and retrieving his own pass
 (ii) introduce shoulder pass with a bounce, as this allows controlled power to be used

2 *Two players per ball*
 (i) simple passing and catching in pairs using all passes (photo 26)
 (ii) bounce passing using shoulder pass; the controlled rebound from the floor can easily be directed high, low and wide to reinforce catching techniques.
 (iii) players pass the ball continuously to each other at walking and running speeds, going both forwards and backwards, staying equidistant from each other at all times
 (iv) shoulder passes with the forearm of the passing arm being held as described previously
 (v) long throws between each other the length of the court. The *leg muscles* are used to give the ball height and distance; exclusive use of the arm, wrist and fingers only can cause the ball to screw off to the side

3 *Three players per ball*
 (i) players stand in triangle formation passing the ball round and across
 (ii) as above except that the pass has to be disguised and executed at varying speeds

Photo 24 ▲                    Photo 25 ▼

Photo 26 ▼

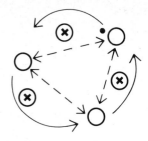

Figure 32

(iii) three cones are placed in a triangle formation (figure 32). Players run round the cones passing the ball on the move. Repeat
several times changing direction and speed. In addition a
bench may be added over which players must leap to jump
pass; also players can zig-zag through cones across the court to
simulate change of pace and direction as in game situation.

## 4  *Group passing in lines*

Figure 33

*Figure 33*: players are divided into two groups of six facing each
other 5 to 10 metres apart. Player A passes to player C and goes to
the end of his line; C passes to B, etc. Practise mainly the shoulder
pass.

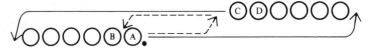

Figure 34

*Figure 34*: in a game situation the shoulder pass is used by players
moving at speed. Thus the same practice as above is carried out at
the fastest possible tempo. Player A runs with the ball and passes to
C who is already on the move. A goes to the end of C's line. C,
having taken the pass, runs and passes to B, etc.

 (i) practise major passes in sequence – shoulder pass, cross-body
and side wrist pass. From time to time introduce the jump
pass, bounce pass and chest pass
 (ii) repeat with passes mixed and speed of players varied

(iii) introduce a competitive element where there is more than one set of lines

There are at least three different ways of introducing competition into passing practices; competition gives purpose and enjoyment as well as heightening interest:
  (i) number of passes executed within a set time limit, e.g. 3 minute period with deductions for dropped passes
 (ii) first to reach a prearranged total without a mistake, for instance, 30 consecutive passes
(iii) highest number of passes until a mistake

## 5 *Zigzag passing in lines*

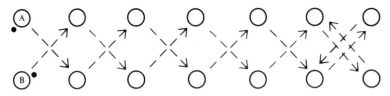

Figure 35

*Figure 35*: players are arranged in two lines each player 5 metres distant from opposite number and from own team-mate. Players A and B have a ball. Passes are criss-crossed up the lines and back.

## 6 *Passing in lines across the hall*

Figure 36

Figure 36 shows starting position of players.
  (i) ball passed left to right by side wrist pass
 (ii) ball passed right to left by cross-body pass
(iii) as above except that the players walk/jog/ run forward as they pass
(iv) each player catches the pass, sprints three steps, passes and retreats to his original spot
 (v) each player receives his pass, sprints three steps, turns, bounces and passes before returning to his starting position
(vi) repeat of (v) except that the player jump passes

## 7  *Passing in circles*

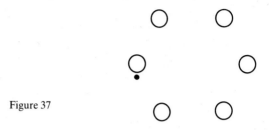

Figure 37

Figure 37 shows starting position of players.
  (i)  passing the ball around the circle using lateral passes
 (ii)  shoulder passing back and forwards across the circle
(iii)  all the players moving together forwards or backwards whilst passing
 (iv)  one player stands in the circle centre passing to any player of his choice and receiving the return pass
  (v)  the centre player has the ball, runs to any player on the circumference, passes the ball to him and takes his place; this player receives the pass, runs across to another player then takes his place and so on
 (vi)  repeat except players running with the ball must take three steps, bounce and pass
(vii)  introduce a second ball. The centre player has a ball as well as a player on the perimeter. The centre player passes in and out at random receiving his outward pass on return. Increase tempo as handling improves

**Passing practices – elementary to advanced**

*Figure 38*: (i) A runs with ball at defender B and jump passes to C. A takes B's position whilst B runs to A's original position. (ii) C now has the ball and runs to jump pass over A who moves to C's original position. (iii) B with the ball, etc.

*Figure 39*: A passes to C, runs behind F. C passes to E, runs behind B. E passes to B, runs behind D, etc.

*Figure 40*: A passes to D, runs towards C, receives return pass, passes to C and takes up C's position. C passes to E, runs towards B, receives return pass, passes to B and takes up B's position, etc.

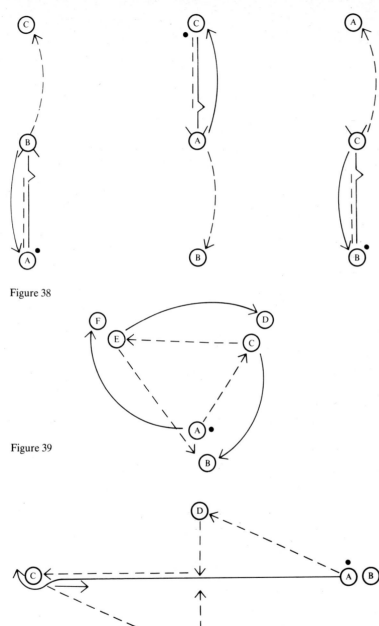

Figure 38

Figure 39

Figure 40

*Figure 41*: A runs, receives pass from F and returns it, receives pass from G and returns it, etc.

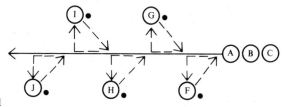

Figure 41

*Figure 42*: A runs and passes to B, runs behind D. B runs and passes to E, etc.

Figure 42

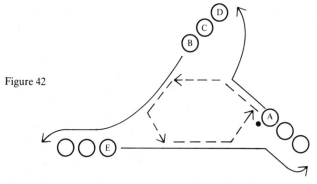

Three further self-explanatory drills are illustrated below in figs 43, 44 and 45.

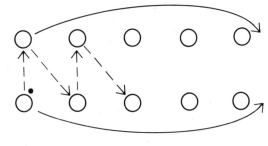

Figure 43

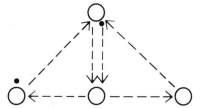

Figure 44

Figure 45

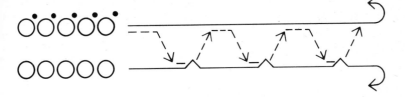

# 6 Principles and practice of shooting

Handball is a sport which revolves round the scoring of goals. Both players and spectators thrive when goals are being scored at both ends in fast, dynamic and spectacular fashion. With an approximate average of around 40 goals per game handball can be considered a high-scoring sport. Although all players must have the ability to take advantage of scoring chances the backs represent the core of a team's shooting power and all successful teams are built round these strong distance shooters. The other players work individually or collectively on tactical moves designed to weaken the defence and to set up scoring opportunities for these trained specialists. Power, speed, accuracy and timing are the qualities common to the top-class shooters who also possess in varying degrees quickness of thought and action, opportunism, manoeuvrability, vision, anticipation, instinct, desire, single-mindedness and the ability to survive often-harsh physical challenges.

## Shoulder shot

The shoulder shot is the simplest and most natural method of shooting the ball for goal. It is the shot most favoured by beginners who, in their formative years, develop the movement through a number of related activities such as the throwing of tennis and cricket balls, snowballs, stones, etc. See photos 27 and 28.

The shot may be executed in a static position or, in its more effective form, at speed as the shooter sprints in towards the 9 metre line. Its mechanical advantages allow maximum power, the force coming from the strong leg muscles being transferred from a wide base through hips, trunk, shoulder, arm and, finally, the wrist. (The incredible throwing power of the javelin thrower illustrates the limit to which this particular movement can be developed.) The shoulder shot can be executed with a high degree of precision but

Photo 27

Photo 28

this is offset by the relatively long wind-up which permits defenders increased reaction time to block the shot. Another consideration to take into account is the decrease in the shot's effectiveness at advanced levels – the ball, at its point of rear extremity (i.e. the point at which it is held furthest back in the shooter's hand prior to release) travels in basically one plane, thereby allowing defenders time to anticipate its flight path. The goalkeeper, for the same reason, has relatively little difficulty in narrowing down possible lines of travel for the ball. Instead of holding the ball far back in its classical shooting position some coaches are now teaching players to hold the ball further forward close to the head, sacrificing power for speed in an attempt to overcome the opposition's 'reading' of this shot.

The shoulder shot is best executed by a shooter advancing in on the defence; when he gets as close to the 9 metre line as possible he checks his speed with a long last stride to widen his throwing base as he enters the shooting position. A right hander will put his left foot forward pointing towards the goal. His left leg is flexed with the trailing right leg reasonably straight. The ball is held in the palm of the right hand with the shooting arm high, flexed and well back. The left arm is bent across the chest and the left shoulder points in the throwing direction. This position is the same as for the shoulder pass (figure 46). The total power of the shot is transmitted from the legs through to the throwing hand and is assisted by the player pressing his left foot down into the floor (photo 27). The final wrist flick adds a late change of direction if a defender or the goalkeeper moves quickly in anticipation offering a potential block. The shot should be directed towards the top corners of the goal (photo 28) or, occasionally, close to the goalkeeper's head. The effectiveness

Figure 46

of the shot in top-class handball is now diminishing but for novices it should be the basic shooting method until the jump shot is perfected.

## Jump shot

Once mastered this shot is the most effective shot in the game, not solely on the basis of the number of goals scored but also on the options and possibilities which develop when a player threatens danger from a jump-shot position. See figure 47.

 Figure 47

In the early stages beginners find it awkward to learn and many are put off and discouraged by their inability to jump vertically. For the execution of the jump shot, rhythm is the most important single factor, beginning with a secure catch of the ball at speed, through to the take-off, into the jump, up into the shooting position, the actual shot itself and the conclusion with a sound (safe) landing. Although the potential force of the shot is not as great as in the shoulder shot the shooter 'in the air' has a number of advantages:

  (i) from the beginning of the wind-up to the release the ball in the shooter's hand travels in a number of planes which can upset the goalkeeper's judgement

 (ii) the attacker can change the shot's direction at the last moment by turning his shoulder and arm

(iii) he can aim the ball to bounce off the floor to pass over or beyond the goalkeeper's leg (photo 29)

(iv) being high up in the air the jump shooter is in a strong 'psycho-logical' position vis-à-vis the defenders and the keeper

The shot, for a right hander, begins when he controls the ball securely in both hands from a pass directed at him as he advances at speed towards the 9 metre line, where he will normally be challenged by an on-coming defender. He then takes a long last stride, planting his leading foot out, pressing his body weight on to the floor and jumps vertically into the air raising his left arm to improve the mechanical efficiency of the jump (figure 48). The jump shooter will drive in from the left and jump with as little horizontal movement as possible to reduce the risk of injury with defenders. When high up in the shooting position the rotation of the upper body and shoulders allows more power to be added. Care must be taken to extend the flexed right knee which helps the height of the jump at take-off. If it remains in this high position the referee may blow for dangerous play. As the shooter advances the ball is carried in two hands, but it is transferred into the shooting hand at take-off. Total control of the ball is necessary as the ball is moved into the shooting position where it is held in the palm of the hand with the arm held high and as far back as mobility allows. Quite often players, at the height of the jump, hang back and delay the shot fractionally, releasing it as the outstretched arms of the defenders are being lowered. The target should be one of the four corners of the goal. If one particular jump shooter is dominating play then he should be marked on a man-to-man basis. Defenders must look out for jump shooters who advance with changes of pace and direction and should remember to block any left-handed shooters on the correct side. Often players in the jump-shot position can be used for 'taking out' defenders, i.e. jumping up, then feeding the ball like lightning to a better-placed colleague as the defence is partially drawn out of position.

Photo 29

Figure 48

**6 metre jump or break shot**

This shot is similar to the 9 metre jump shot but is different on three counts:

(i)   it is executed from the 6 metre line
(ii)  there is no defence to jump over as the shooting player is in the clear
(iii) it is a horizontal jump

This shot is commonly used to finish off a fast break following a quick throw from the keeper or gaining breakaway possession through interception. The attacker has only the goalkeeper to beat. He receives the ball on the break, runs and dribbles the ball towards the 6 metre line judging his approach to the line, then takes off and jumps as far as he can towards the goal to shoot past the keeper at point-blank range. He should rarely miss from this situation.

Photo 30

**Fall shot and dive shot**

The basis of both shots is the same, the dive shot being an extension of the fall shot. When the fall shot (photo 30) is used the shooter has one foot in contact with the floor as close to the 6 metre line as possible. In the dive shot (photo 31) the player dives through the air into the goal area to shoot from the closest possible range (remembering, as already pointed out, that the body must be clear of the ground until the ball is released).

Very few players new to handball will try the fall or dive shots naturally, and care must be taken to introduce selected progressions which will reduce any apprehensions and possible injury. Both these shots are attempted by line players who receive a pass as they move around the 6 metre line probing for gaps and scoring opportunities. The pass is caught in two hands close to the chest and the player falls forward, quickly pivoting on his left foot to shoot. As he

Photo 31

performs the shot the left shoulder leads and the ball is held securely at the chest for as long as possible to minimize the chances of being dispossessed. It is an advantage for a right-handed player to receive the pass when drifting round the 6 metre line from left to right (and vice versa for left handers).

The fall and dive shots are absolutely fundamental for players playing in and behind the opposing defence on the 6 metre line. Such players must be fast, good catchers of a ball and, ideally, stockily built to enable them to maintain their momentum as they drive off the ground to shoot. They must be prepared to soak up a lot of physical contact and need an abundance of courage as the possibility of injury during the execution of the shot is always present especially in the event of some late ill-timed tackles in mid-air.

Beginners require special consideration in the initial practices where mats should be used to soften landings. Players should be taught the correct recovery method where one or both hands break the fall and the shooter rolls round to regain his feet quickly as in volleyball. The use of kneepads is recommended at all levels for protection.

**Other shots**

There are a number of other shots in addition to the basic examples just described; they are executed in certain circumstances according to the level and experience of the players involved. The following are an example of some of them, listed in order of popularity in schools and club handball.

*Low shot*

The shooter advances in towards the 9 metre line in preparation for a shoulder shot but at the last moment decides to shoot low under the upraised arms of a defender. This shot is not particularly effective against talented defenders but is useful at lower levels where defenders tend to forget to lower their hands in anticipation of low shots. It can really only be tried a few times in a game. In order for the shooter to fire the ball at its lowest point he extends the foot of his leading leg in a long last stride, sinks low with his hips and lets the ball go at around knee height (figure 49). The ball is directed into the bottom corners often with a bounce. Again, the final wrist flick allows for split-second last-minute changes of direction.

Figure 49

*Side shot*

Instead of shooting high or low to beat the defence the attacker may decide to fire the ball round the side of the covering players. A right hander will pretend to shoot to the defender's left but suddenly raise his right leg, moving his body to the left and pivoting on his left foot (photo 32 and figure 50). As he falls to the side he twists, his body and shoulders, bringing the ball round low and held out to shoot for goal under and round the defender's arms, giving himself space for additional sight of the goal. The shot can be most effective if performed in moderation with an element of surprise. Wingers sometimes use it to widen their shooting angle, e.g. a left hander in the left-hand corner. A more effective and advanced version can be employed with the attacker diving to the side instead of falling.

*Hip shot*

This is an effective shot which requires great practice; the attacker receives the ball, holds it at hip height, then suddenly whips the ball for goal (photo 33). The wind-up and preparation are very rapid in comparison to the shoulder shot. The actual flight path of the ball is

Figure 50

Photo 32

Photo 33

difficult for defenders to determine as the shot is snapped out and is sometimes used to beat goalkeepers when they are unsighted. The firer flexes his knees as he shoots and the ball goes under defenders' arms. Often the shooter falls away to the right side as he releases this shot.

*Penalty*

This shot from the 7 metre penalty line is governed by one important rule: the foot of the shooter cannot break contact with the floor (figure 51). A version of the fall shot is, therefore, usually used or often as in soccer, the shooter picks a spot and 'blasts it'. If the keeper advances out too far, however, a lob can be a fruitful alternative. The penalty taker should observe the weight distribution of the goalkeeper and look for premature movement of the feet. It is better to have someone other than the player involved in the award taking the throw as this particular player may throw hurriedly or recklessly in anger or frustration and is best given time to regain composure.

Figure 51

*Lob*

The lob is used to beat a keeper who has advanced too far out of his goal; there are at least three occasions when this is likely:
  (i) when he stands too far out to narrow the angle of a penalty throw
 (ii) when he rushes out to smother a line player who has received a pass with his back turned to goal and is in the process of turning to shoot
(iii) when he goes out to narrow the angles for a player on the fast break

*Reverse shot*

When a player receives the ball with his back to goal he can shoot immediately, saving vital precious seconds which he would require to turn and face the goal. The ball is caught in two hands and transferred to the throwing hand whilst still in front of the body. The shooter then moves the ball out from his body with fingers open and propels it vigorously backwards using as much wrist power as he can muster in an attempt to take the goalkeeper by surprise. The reverse shot is not recommended for beginners and is only used by experienced performers in very exceptional circumstances. It should *never* be used as a substitute for one of the standard throws.

Some top-level performers develop shots of their own but they are infrequently used and can be classed as 'personal idiosyncrasies' and, as such, are not included here.

**Lead-up procedures, progressions and practices for shooting**

*Shoulder shot*

Having explained and demonstrated the correct technique, position the players in lines with the front players standing on the 9 metre line facing the goal. Instruct the front players to stand in the stance for the execution of a static shoulder shot. Go round each in turn correcting the technique, ensuring the ball is resting in the palm of the shooting hand and that the opposite foot is forward. Concentrate on the use of the wrist and instruct as follows (sequences in figure 52):

Figure 52

  (i)  keeping both feet on the ground, shoot to hit the bar
 (ii)  holding the forearm of the shooting arm with the opposite hand, shoot using wrist power only to hit the bar
(iii)  releasing wrist move the lines back so that the shot is executed following one step
(iv)  repeat the same shot following three steps
 (v)  move lines back, each player with a ball throwing it up to let it bounce, catching it, taking three steps and shooting
(vi)  repeat except shoot following three sprinted steps

Add goalkeepers and defenders as required according to progression rate.

*Jump shot*

After explanation and demonstration, position players in lines as for the shoulder shot with the leaders about 4 metres outside the 9 metre line. Instruct as follows:

  (i)  each in turn runs to the 9 metre line and jumps as high as possible with the take-off foot planted on the line. Right handers jump off the left foot and vice versa. (This might be, at first, unnatural for some who have a preferred jumping foot as in high jumping or hurdling take-off.) Eliminate the 'long jump' and encourage the players to land close to their take-off points; continue until all the players use the correct take-off foot. Criticize and advise as required
 (ii)  repeat with players raising both arms as they jump
(iii)  repeat with only the shooting arm raised – emphasize height

(iv) repeat with left shoulder turned towards goal, the shooting arm slightly flexed and extended back

(v) repeat with lines angled towards goal – right handers coming in from the left. Now introduce a ball which is raised to the shooting position but not released

(vi) repeat with the coach standing and jumping up as a defender. Players holding a ball must jump and hit the trainer's upstretched hand

(vii) as above without the coach with the players now shooting for goal with and without bounce as required (as in sequences in figure 53)

(viii) emphasize use of wrist and ask players to enter the 'hang' phase where they lean back and delay their shot

At this stage where the shots are being executed unopposed, practices can be made more realistic by adding:

(i) a goalkeeper

(ii) a bench on the 9 metre line over which shooters must jump

(iii) an active defender

(iv) a bar or piece of elastic over which shooter must lift hand to shoot down for goal

Encourage the players to aim for the four corners and stand behind the keeper pointing at spots in the goal at which you may wish the shots to be directed.

Figure 53

*Fall shot and dive shot*

To reduce apprehension and possible injury initial practices should be done in a kneeling position. Divide the class into threes, two kneeling opposite each other with the third collecting stray balls. Change over every so often.

   (i)  shoulder pass to each other in kneeling position with the body upright (photo 34)
 (ii)  repeat with fall forward after pass
(iii)  repeat with left arm breaking the fall
(iv)  repeat with roll round on the right shoulder on the floor
 (v)  repeat with players in a crouched position balancing on their toes

Figure 54

(vi) repeat from standing through the crouch position
(vii) repeat adding a twist with the final shot

To create the game situation, position all the players round the 6 metre line each with a ball (or sharing balls). Position mats for landing on:

(i) kneel and shoot
(ii) squat, shoot, roll
(iii) stand, squat, shoot, roll, regain feet
(iv) stand, shoot, roll, regain feet (see fig. 54)

Add the goalkeeper and place the players in groups of six round the 6 metre line. The group which scores the most shots is the winner. Encourage players to shoot high and low with bounces. An alternative method often more suitable for adult beginners is, having demonstrated the shot, position players on the 6 metre line beside each other and proceed as follows:

(i) each in turn facing the goal falls forward and breaks fall with hands and arms
(ii) as above with the fall being broken by outstretched left hand while the right arm is held bent in the shooting position
(iii) the same but going through the motions of shooting

Photo 34

(iv)  repeat with a slight twist and delay
 (v)  the same with the introduction of a ball as well as an active goalkeeper
(vi)  repeat with inactive, then active, defenders with the shooters being fed passes from the trainer or other players on the 9 metre line
(vii)  instruct players to *dive* instead of fall to ascertain, at this early stage, if there are any promising dive shooters for the future

### Low shot

Develop as with shoulder shot progressions. Position of defenders is best if there are two standing beside each other with their hands linked low, leaving a gap under which the shooter must release the ball. Alternatively the coach can stand side on to the 9 metre line holding a towel or tracksuit top under which the shots must be aimed. This shot should also be practised with a fall (sequences in figure 55).

### Hip shot

Practices and progressions are the same as for the shoulder and low shots.

### Side shot

This shot is best practised in pairs where each player in turn acts as shooter and defender. The defender stands on the 9 metre line with his arms held in the typical defensive stance (page 128). The shooter stands one pace adrift and steps forward as if to shoulder shoot to his right. Without the ball at first, the shooter dummies to shoot high but lifts his right leg and, as he falls to the left, shoots. The players should practise the shot with a twist and delay before utilizing a ball. Encourage attackers to run in three steps and side shoot both from in front of the goal and from the wings. Add a keeper and make the defender as active as required. Finish progressions with attackers driving goalwards in lines as with the previous shots and when they reach the defenders on the 9 metre line they can select which shot they wish to use in an attempt to deceive the custodian. Figure 55 illustrates the sequences involved.

Figure 55

### 6 metre jump shot

By now progressions should be fairly self-evident for players and coaches alike. For this particular shot one practice is especially useful and is commonly used for the fast break (page 115).

Position the players in a single line on their defending 9 metre line each with a ball; as they sprint up the court they pass to the coach and receive his return pass on the halfway line. The players then have to continue for goal at speed controlling the ball, ensuring they do not double dribble, take four strides or foul the 6 metre line before shooting.

*Penalty shot*

At the conclusion of each training session the trainer organizes competitions amongst the players. He can, if he wishes, stand behind the keeper indicating at the last moment where he wants the shot directed.

## Shooting practices in diagrams

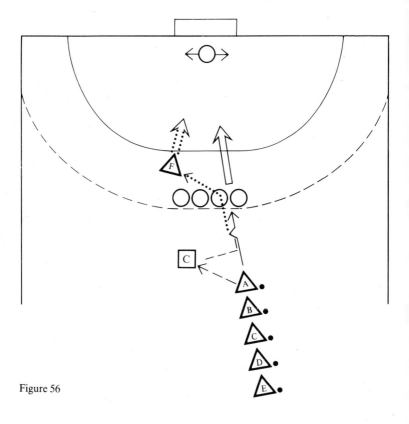

Figure 56

*Figure 56*: the players line up A to E as shown. A passes to the coach, runs forward for the return and tries to jump shoot over the defenders who are lined up on the free throw line. He may use team-mate F to deceive the opposition by jump passing the ball just before attempting to shoot. He then collects the ball and joins end of line whilst B goes into action (and so on).

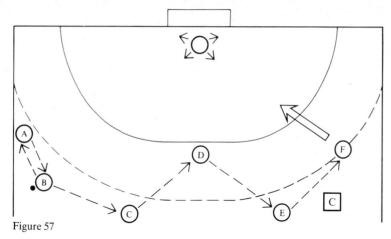

Figure 57

*Figure 57*: players pass the ball around and decide at will when to shoot. Keeper must cover all possible angles including player D. The sequence is B–A–B–C–D–E–F who shoots. Coach may also call the letter of player to shoot on his next receipt of the ball.

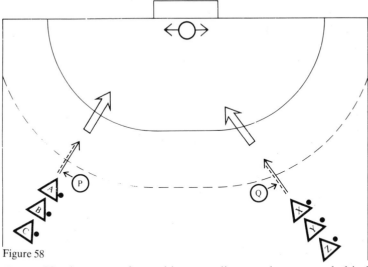

Figure 58

*Figure 58*: players are formed into two lines as shown, one behind A, one behind X and each with a ball. Players come in alternately from each side shooting in rapid succession before re-joining their line. Defenders P and Q make minimal efforts in defence, merely serving to keep the shooting angle from narrowing.

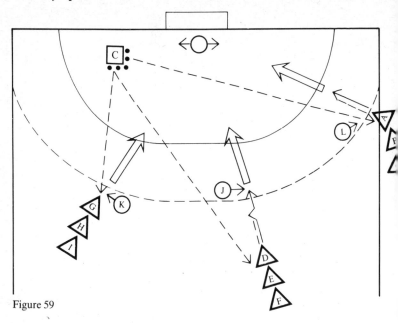

Figure 59

*Figure 59*: the three-pronged attack. The coach passes the ball to the front member of each of the three lines. A shoots from the wing D jump shoots over defender J – G shoots any way he wants. K, J and L are 'floating' defenders in this exercise so the method of shooting (and the sequence) can be altered as required.

Figures 60, 61 and 62 illustrate three further self-explanatory drills.

Figure 60

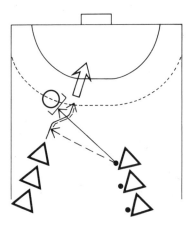

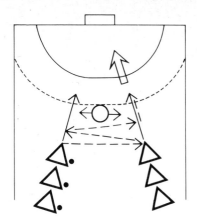

Figure 61

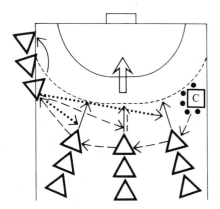

Figure 62

# 7 Goalkeeping

In handball the goalkeeper is the last line of defence and, thus, the significance of his position needs no underlining. Compared with some other sports where it is the function of a keeper to protect a goal, the handball goalkeeper is required to exercise a far more complex range of skills than his counterparts. Handball's last line is called upon to react, anticipate, think, concentrate, outmanoeuvre, direct and organize continuously throughout a match at an extremely fast rate. The goalkeeper is often acknowledged as being the most important single player in the handball team.

For the coach it is often heartbreaking to organize a handball team, train them to master basic skills, instil a high degree of perfection in the knowledge and execution of attacking and defensive systems, only to lose vital matches because of the lack of a good keeper. The physical qualities demanded for the goalkeeping position are such that suitable aspirants are not easy to find; ideally, they should be tall, loose-limbed (mobile and flexible) with long arms and legs, physically strong and fearless with fast reflex actions and the ability to move sharply over short distances. The physical attributes must be matched with powers of intense mental application in a game where any lapse of concentration can be particularly disastrous.

Keepers are usually talented at other ball games and should be encouraged to participate in such other sports not only for general enjoyment but to assist in the development of their own particular training. Table tennis, for example, would be a simple relaxing, yet beneficial, activity for reflex training.

Soccer goalkeepers, in general, have not been found to be good handball keepers and vice versa; the soccer goalie moves for the ball in an entirely different manner to save shots. The footballer adopts a crouch position more often and saves many shots by diving and throwing his body long distances across his goal. The handball

Photo 35

custodian, however, remains upright (photo 35) and stops the opposition's attempts by quick arm or leg movements – he rarely dives
as in football. He has to work continuously in a game and is called
upon to save shots several times each minute; the soccer keeper can
go for long periods without any activity and is sometimes called
upon to concentrate only in spasmodic bursts. The handball keeper
is also the initiator of attacks leading to the scoring of goals through
fast breaks. As well as saving shots he must do so in such a way that
he can release the ball into play as quickly as possible; all shots
should be saved or parried, the ball being brought under control
quickly. For example, a high shot to the top-left-hand corner of the
goal should be saved by an extension of the left arm accompanied
by a forward, downward rotation of the arm to direct the ball
towards the floor to be caught following the bounce and passed
swiftly and accurately to a colleague en route to the opposition's
goal.

Goalkeepers should wear a heavy jersey with long sleeves. The stinging effect of the ball on skin contact forces the wearing of tracksuit bottoms. Kneepads and, occasionally, elbow pads are worn depending on the technique employed by the goalkeeper concerned. Novices sometimes pad themselves with foam to protect the hips. The most important protective aid for goalkeepers, however, is the 'box' as used by hockey and cricket players. The use of a facemask is becoming more commonplace but is, as yet, still relatively rare. Inexperienced keepers tend to throw themselves about (often to their own discomfort) to a far greater degree than experienced ones who save shots in a balanced sound position with appropriate angles covered correctly. Stopping low shots in the proper 'splits' position (photo 36) the goalkeeper should be able to recover his feet immediately.

The goalkeeper is given a favoured place within the rules of handball. He may play the ball with his feet, is not limited to a specific number of steps with the ball and can play outside his area as an outfield player (but not cross the halfway line). Unlike his soccer counterpart he can deflect the ball over the back line yet still retain possession without conceding a corner. Carrying the ball outside of, or back into, his own area, however, results in the award of a penalty.

When the opposition have possession and are engaged in attacking tactical moves, the goalkeeper must concentrate on the movement of the ball and of the opposition players in relation to his own defenders. To do this he must understand how defensive systems operate against various attacking moves. While the ball is being played around by opponents he must shout instructions to his defenders to ensure that they adhere to the correct principles of defence; if, for example, a defender fails to move out to the 9 metre line to stop an attacker's advance he may well be allowing a clear shot at goal. In theory goalkeepers should stop all shots from the 9 metre line; stopping a shot from closer than this distance is considered a bonus. They should warn their defence of unmarked line players who may be drifting into open spaces on the 6 metre line in anticipation of a feed from a colleague. It is absolutely essential that the goalkeeper can spot weaknesses in his team's defence, responding instantly with appropriate constructive criticism and instructions to players concerned.

As the opposition move the ball around in attacking moves the goalkeeper, as well as supervising his defensive set-up, must follow

Photo 36

the path of the ball, especially when it comes close to the 9 metre free throw line: this is the danger point. At all times he must be positioned *directly between the ball and the goal* and at an *angle* which makes the attacker's *view of the goal minimal* thereby giving the goal *maximum protection*. As the ball travels across from left to right he corresponds swiftly by taking rapid, short, balanced sidesteps. During this period his 'arc of cover' begins with him being jammed against his left post on the goal line; from there, following the movement of the ball, he will move out and round in a semi-circular path being, at the maximum, about 1 metre out from the centre of his goal, before moving back on the curved path to his right-hand post (figure 63). The top and bottom corners of the goal are his main weak spots at which opponents will aim, quite often, particularly fierce shots; by moving out slightly he may lessen the target area for such shots. The one danger of this forward movement, however, is the subsequent reduction in reaction time required to block such a shot. The actual distance of the forward advance is a matter of individual interpretation according to physical attributes, reaction time and the speed, power and accuracy of

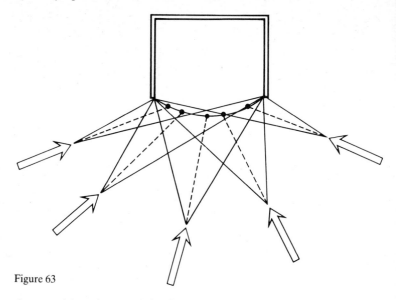

Figure 63

the attacking shooters. As the goalkeeper follows this arc he must continue to hold his arms high and be in a position for any sudden instant reaction required on his part; if his arms drop due to fatigue, or lack of concentration, an alert shooter may only require this split second to capitalize on the chance. The arm action serves an additional function – that of establishing a sound position. For instance, when playing against a swift-moving team who interchange players, pace and direction constantly, he will be under constant stress being forced to move from side to side, out and back, many times; as his concentration on the ball is so intense he may well lose his sense of position (punishable again by astute attackers) and this, in fact, is what quite often happens to inexperienced players. He does not have the time to look round or assess his position by looking at floor markings. He can, therefore, use his arms to touch bar and posts, especially the top junctions, to re-establish himself into the best possible positions.

Anticipation, developed through experience (and quite often mistakes!), plays a more important part in a keeper's performance in handball than in soccer. A thorough knowledge of attacking principles, especially in relation to the movement of line players, means a goalkeeper can move smartly out to the 6 metre line to surprise a line player who has received a feed and is in the process of turning round to shoot. Again some teams have excellent shooters who are, however, often limited to one good shot, for instance the jump shot. During the opposition warm-up the goalkeeper should attempt to study just who the powerful shooters are, what shots they look likely to excel at, where they like shooting – high, low, right, left, etc. The first ten minutes or so should confirm many of his suspicions. To dent the confidence of a good jump shooter who shoots with a bounce, a good low save in the opening minutes could prove vital. If an attacker likes shooting high the keeper can tempt an early shot by dropping his arms to entice such an attempt before reacting *and* saving instantly. Also, players with poor low shots can be tempted to shoot low by instructing the defence to fail to block a certain player's attempt. Goalkeepers can, in effect, deceive shooters by moving fractionally to one side before the ball leaves the hand and then moving back as the shot is released. Similarly, a keeper can stand off centre deliberately to tempt shots or intentionally show a gap between himself and the near upright to attacks from the wings, inviting shots which can then be saved by the 'advanced' anticipation.

The vital commodity of anticipation is acquired through experience and by discussion with, and playing amongst, good players. At training the keeper can question the shooters on their favourite shots, what they look for in a goalkeeper, how they spot his weaknesses, what type of goalie is hardest to beat, etc. In addition it is sometimes desirable for the goalkeeper to play outfield in practice matches so that he can come to understand how a shooter's mind works and to study, from his point of view, how goalkeepers react to varying situations. A good goalkeeper should always appreciate the opportunity of experiencing shooting.

In handball a keeper should save about 50 per cent of all shots directed at goal (excluding those blocked by defenders); it must be stated, however, that it is incorrect to judge a keeper by the number of shots saved. The really good goalkeeper is the one who, by excellent positioning, *prevents* an attacker from *attempting* to shoot at goal. Very often less able keepers who fail in this respect are made to look better than they actually are simply because they have been called upon to save a shot that the real class player would have prevented happening in the first place. Also, a good goalkeeper will look relaxed and make the stopping of shots look easy whilst the less able may make the stopping of simple shots look spectacular.

As the opposition play the ball around, the goalkeeper gears himself to be ready to act when a shooter moves to the 9 metre line. He adopts a basic stance, balancing himself, feet about 18 inches apart, weight on the balls of the feet, legs slightly flexed and body upright. His head is held high and the eyes are always focussed on the ball. The arms are flexed and are either held close to the head or at the 90 degree angle (photo 35). This latter position allows quicker coverage of the top corners but could be susceptible to a shot close to the ears which top-class keepers have been known to save with their heads! It is a matter of trial and error and individual preference as to which style is adopted. Irrespective of style it must be re-emphasized that at all times the *eyes are on the ball*. If a keeper moves too soon the shooter can re-direct the ball to the resultant gaps created by the premature move. When the shooter does release the ball the keeper must respond – the success of this response depends on his reaction time and his technique, a technique which is learned and developed by coaching and playing experience. As well as stopping the ball the keeper and his team-mates are fully aware of the possibilities of initiating an attack if the ball can be brought under control and released back into play constructively. To catch a shot is, of course, the ideal but this seldom happens. The keeper tries to cushion the power of the ball by killing it so that it drops to the floor to be received quickly on the rebound and returned into play with a throw of up to 30 metres in a fast break. In training, the goalkeeper should practise killing the ball with his arms, body, and even his legs. If he is under stress from a powerful and accurate shot a deflection past the post or over the bar would suffice as possession of the ball returns to him; deflections back into play, however, are very dangerous as alert line players are always waiting to snap up such chances.

The goalkeeper's points of vulnerability are the top and bottom corners. To save in the top two corners he will extend his respective arms combined with a slight push off the feet (photo 37). Thus, there is nothing very complicated about high corner shots. Low shots to the bottom corners are a different matter and are extremely difficult to save especially those which bounce as they come in towards goal. The keeper, in this case, has to extend his appropriate foot outwards passing through the splits position (photo 36). A keeper able to get down quickly into this position will save many such shots but to stop the bouncing ones he must also reach out with his arm, and this requires a great deal of technical training. Often it is not enough to get down and save the ball; he must be able to get back up on to his feet quickly to save any possible rebound shot. For

Photo 37

a goalkeeper to adopt a good wide splits position requires constant mobility work in the hip, adductor and hamstring regions and it is not enough to undertake such mobility work only at training sessions. The coach must ensure that the goalkeeper works through a series of mobility exercises over a long period at home and may advise him to attend an athletics club to train with high jumpers and hurdlers or work with the local gymnastics club. The correct 'passive' method of stretching muscles must be fully understood and a knowledge of the treatment of muscle and tendon injuries acquired. The adductor longus and hamstring tendons are particularly susceptible to recurrent injury if flexibility work is not adequately sustained on a regular basis.

Shots coming in from wing positions are saved by a *puppet-like* movement. The keeper stands against the near post with his weight on the foot nearest the post (photo 38). By holding the inside arm high, covering the junction of the bar and near post, he leaves no gaps on that particular side. This forces the shooter to aim for the other, open, side of the goal with either a high or a low shot. High shots will be stopped by the outstretched arm and low ones by the

Photo 38

Photo 39

corresponding leg movement (photo 39). Shots coming in at around hip height will be saved by the *arm* moving *downwards* and the *leg* moving *upwards*. Both these limbs are 'free-swinging' as the bulk of the body weight is on the leg at the near post. If the winger is permitted a run-in before shooting the keeper could advance outwards directly at the shooter almost in the same stance. Before play begins the goalkeeper should get his own wingers to practise wing shots so that he is aware of the scoring angles which might conceivably be remembered by association with marks on the wall or other such landmarks. Wingers, when they shoot, often spin the ball but, nevertheless, it is important for the keeper to have his eyes glued to it every time.

When an opposing line player receives a feed on the 6 metre line the goalkeeper has at least three options when attempting to block the resultant shot. If the line player receives the ball while facing away from the goal he has to turn before shooting; this allows the keeper time to rush out to smother the shot. He then becomes vulnerable to the lob over his head. Instead he may decide to come off his line and form himself into a star jump position (photo 40) or, as another alternative, may advance a little and split in anticipation of a low shot. All he can really do is narrow the angles and cover as large an area as he possibly can.

Photo 40

A penalty shot from the 7 metre line again raises the question of how far a keeper can advance in relation to his reaction time. It is recognized that he *must* advance for the penalty and some choose around 3 metres as being the optimum distance to come forward. Again, anticipation, experience and reaction time are the deciding factors.

When the goalkeeper faces an opponent sprinting in to the 6 metre line in a fast break it is probably best for him to go out at the same speed as the attacker is advancing. Often the star jump position with moving arms and legs or a crucifix position with a slight jump are effective. To remain on the goal line is useless. Star jump positions, however, are vulnerable to a bouncing ball.

## Training

Training for the goalkeeper involves participation in the general training required by the rest of the team as well as very specialist work related to his own physical conditioning and particular skill development. In the latter he may work separately from his teammates quite frequently. His training, therefore, can be divided into three sections, general physical conditioning, mobility work, and skill training.

## General physical conditioning

This is dealt with in the chapter on training methods. In this instance the goalkeeper joins in with the rest of the team.

## Mobility work

The goalkeeper must develop a high degree of flexibility particularly in the trunk, hip and leg regions before any attempt can be made to develop correct technique. Consequently he must apply himself intelligently over a long period of time to a routine of mobility exercises. The coach may find it useful to send him to a gymnastics, ballet or athletics trainer initially so that he can undertake such work in capable hands. At all times during mobility work, relaxation and control must be the norm and the keeper should do his exercises in the peace and quiet of his home environment. The correct stretching procedures should be observed to improve performance and to avoid injury which can sometimes be severe and often recurrent. It is recommended, therefore, that the goalkeeper does his flexibility work at home. Before commencing any stretching movements it is wise to warm up 'loosely' by easy bouncing, running on the spot, skipping, etc.

As already mentioned, the main regions to be thoroughly mobilized are *trunk, hips* and *legs*, especially the hamstring and adductor muscles. The following exercises (which are by no means exhaustive) should give some idea of the type of work required.

1 *Photo 41*: stand relaxed, feet 12 inches apart; stretch down with hands clasped, legs straight, till the furthest depth is reached. Hold for 5 seconds, then gently reach out the hands to touch the floor (aim to brush the palms of the hand on the floor) about twenty times.
2 Same as 1 but with left leg crossed over right (touch floor fifteen times). Change legs and repeat.
3 Start from a standing stance; stretch the right leg back straight and place the left leg forward, flexed at the knee. Place hands on left knee and sit down in that position, gently pressing downwards. Repeat fifteen times then change legs.
4 Lie on back; bend the left knee up to the chest clasping hands round the thigh just behind the knee. Try to straighten the leg without moving the left knee and keeping the right leg completely flat on the floor. Stretch very slowly to maximum then release quickly. Repeat about five times with each leg.

Photo 41

5 *Photo 42*: sit on ground extending left leg out in front; curl the heel of the right foot round against the seat. With shoulders square to the front clasp hands behind the head and gently stretch forward pressing elbows and forehead towards floor. Repeat twenty times then reverse the legs.

6 Adopt a sitting position with legs fully extended in front:
   (i) lean forward easily and touch toes twenty times
   (ii) with elbows clasped behind head press head and elbows towards the knees keeping the legs straight at all times
   (iii) now pull up the knees; grasp heels with hands and place the chin on knees. Keeping the chin on the knees straighten the legs very slowly by pushing out the heels in front. Hold at maximum stretch for five seconds

7 Stand upright and hold a goalpost or other object for support. Keep shoulders square and head high then swing the leg as high forward and as far back to the rear as possible. Again, alternate legs.

8 Face a wallbar, etc. and grasp with both hands. Swing the leg as high as possible to left and right alternately twenty-five times then change legs.

9 Again hold post, etc. for support. Keeping trunk absolutely still and facing directly to the front, raise the outside knee till it is parallel with the ground. Place the free hand inside the knee and ease it round gently as far back as it will go.

10 Place the heel with the leg straight on a firm object (steeple-chase hurdle, box, seat, etc.) about 1 metre in height, the other foot slightly to the rear (make sure the floor surface is firm). Keeping the body upright allow the hips to sink straight down till maximum stretch is felt in the hamstrings behind the thigh. Change legs as required.

11 *Photo 43*: try to adopt a splits position; stretch the heel of the front leg out as far as you can and the toes of the rear leg as far back as you can. This is best done on grass, even better in sand (such as a jumping pit) where the distance between heel and toe can be measured. Try to improve on your personal best distance over a period of time.

12 *Photo 44*: stand with legs as far apart as you can, toes pointing forwards; slide the hands down to grasp the ankles and press head down till it touches the floor. This exercise, and number 11 give a good indication as to a goalkeeper's general degree of mobility.

Photo 42

Photo 43

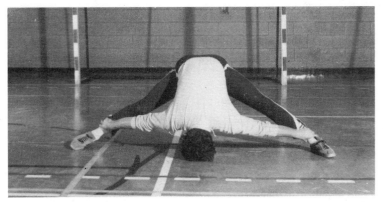

Photo 44

The number of times to do each exercise, as indicated above, is merely a rough guide; exact numbers for full benefit will come to the individual concerned through experience.

Developing a high degree of mobility is in itself, however, not enough. Stretched muscles must be strengthened to prevent injury when called upon to stretch to maximum point of bearance in the game situation, particularly under conditions of fatigue and stress. The use of weights in, for example, the form of anklets may help in this respect. In addition to a thorough warm-up it is beneficial to warm down equally intelligently; this should involve easy running and skipping in relaxed fashion after which a warm bath is ideal.

**Skill training**

This type of training is designed to develop correct technique in the performance of the goalkeeper's skills and includes the knowledge of angles and positioning procedures, the practice of saving shots, the recovery and subsequent use of the ball, initiating attacks (with long throws), improving reaction time and reflexes, developing relaxation and acquiring the confidence so important to the whole team, especially in the defensive situation. Most of his work is done in conjunction with the rest of the team in the form of practices and drills involving the keeper against groups of players shooting or moving around in groups according to a set plan. He can, however, work on his own or, preferably, in partnership with, for example, the reserve keeper.

*Goalkeeper alone*

1 Throws the ball against a wall from varying distances (alternating the power of each throw) trying to catch the ball high, low, to the side, etc.
2 Hits the ball against a wall and tries to prevent the ball from dropping to bounce on the floor by deflecting the ball with his arms.
3 *Photo 45*: using his instep kicks the ball against the wall continuously with alternate feet until it goes out of control.
4 In the manner of the soccer player attempts to keep the ball in the air using both feet ('keepy uppy').
5 Practises sidestepping round his 'arc' from one post to the other, changing pace and direction whilst using his arms to feel for the posts and bar to establish his exact location on the arc.

Photo 45

Photo 46

*With a partner*

1 *Photo 46*: passing the ball to each other at varying heights and directions.
2 Shooting at each other – try to catch the ball cleanly as often as possible.
3 Kicking the ball to each other at close range.

Photo 47

Photo 48

4 *Photo 47*: shoot the ball at hip height so that the shot will be saved in the 'puppet' manner (leg raised to meet lowered arm).

5 Player bounces the ball to partner who is facing in the opposite direction – the latter turns to catch the ball cleanly on hearing the bounce.

6 Player directs a shot at partner which requires a parrying action using body, arms or legs to bring the ball under control quickly.

7 *Photo 48*: the keepers sit on the floor facing each other with legs spread apart as wide as possible; each bounces the ball to his

partner who must save the ball with outstretched hand as the ball bounces over the foot.

8 The player faces a wall about 2 metres out from it; the partner, standing behind him, fires the ball off the wall forcing him to react swiftly to save the rebound. Often the junction of two walls is used. Vary the distance from the wall and the power of the shot.

9 Player throws the ball to his partner below hip height; the partner has to have his hands clasped behind his back forcing a 'feet only' save.

10 Long throws – the keepers practise long throws of up to 40 metres in length from one end of the sports hall to the other. The technique of the long handball throw differs greatly from the short one; the main drive comes from the legs and, once mastered, very accurate throws can be made consistently. Lack of leg drive or over-emphasis on arm power alone often results not only in lack of requisite distance but in a 'screwed' throw which leads to error and, more important, loss of possession.

*With whole team in groups*

This is the part of the goalkeeper's training where his reflexes and reactions will develop and where he will build up his confidence. The coach will select activities to eradicate weaknesses and re-inforce particular strengths. When the shooters are firing at goal the keeper's confidence can be improved, for example, in two ways – the shooters will practise from outside the free throw line so that he saves all their attempts. Gradually, however, the coach moves the shooters closer till he has to *work* to save the shots. Again, if he is weak low down to the left the coach will instruct players to aim for that point until his performance in that particular area shows improvement. At other times the coach may stand behind the goal indicating, as players run in to shoot, at what particular spot he may wish them to aim. A sensible coach should have little difficulty training his keepers; it is a matter of ironing out weaknesses, bolstering strengths, constantly discussing how to improve performance and instilling the correct attitude and appetite for the game.

In team training there are numerous practices (some of which are featured in figures 64, 65 and 66) which the coach may wish to use with particular reference to the goalkeeper. The shooting practices in the previous chapter are equally applicable.

Figure 64

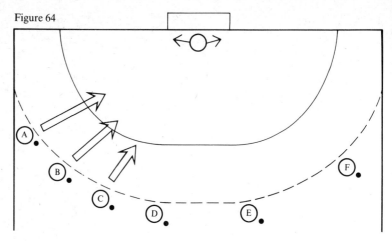

*Figure 64*: the players stand on the 9 metre line, each with a ball in his hand, in sequence A–F as shown:

(i) shoot high
(ii) shoot low
(iii) mixed shot
(iv) shoot at goalkeeper's body (keeper tries to cushion the ball)

The coach decides the intensity and types of shot. The sequence from A to F is maintained all the time.

Figure 65

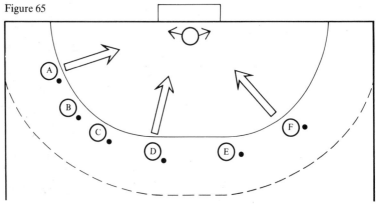

*Figure 65*: players stand on the 6 metre line and fall or dive shoot at goal. The goalkeeper practises the technique of saving such attempts. This time the coach can break the sequence by calling out as required.

Figure 66

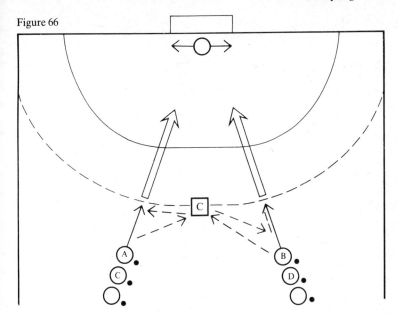

*Figure 66*: two lines of shooters are positioned about 4 metres out from the 9 metre line, as shown. Player A passes the ball to the coach, collects the return, and shoots for goal from the free throw line. B then does the same, then C, then D and so on. On this practice the coach may stand behind the goal with another player taking his place. The coach then gives directions as to where he wants shots placed.

# 8 Principles and practice of play

**Principles of play**

Players can only demonstrate their complete individual skills through an appreciation and understanding of the principles of play. Handball is a team sport which revolves round decisions and the successful team will put together the correct ones.

*Attack*

Ball possession is the foundation of successful attacking play as it permits players time to manoeuvre for shooting chances and engage in individual and collective attacks based on a combination of fast, rapid passing, intelligent positioning and movement and the utilization of offensive techniques and skills. The team with the ball dictates play and denies the opposition time available to score. Positive attacking play is enhanced and reinforced by support, width, mobility, penetration and improvisation.

*Defence*

To neutralize and overcome the attacking qualities of their opponents a team must organize their defensive system to possess width, depth and density. Positive defensive play is the result of support, cover, organization, balance, control and restraint.

The development of attacking and defensive qualities involves speed of thought and action, decision-making and the ability to communicate which can only be learned and acquired by constant pressure practice in improvised training matches and in other correctly structured coaching sessions utilizing a variety of teaching methods, e.g. whole–part–whole, analysis–build-up method, coaching in the game.

The success of any team depends in the final analysis on the quality of the available players. A team plays to its strengths and disguises its weaknesses and is a combination of strength and skill and youth and experience.

## Phases of attacking play

There are four phases to attacking play:

  (i)  the fast break
 (ii)  the extended fast break
(iii)  systems of attack
 (iv)  set pieces

### Fast break

This is the term given to the movement which occurs when a team, gaining possession of the ball, despatch it quickly up court, catching defenders on the turn before they are able to organize their defence. The initial possession in the classical fast-break situation is gained through the goalkeeper parrying the ball and getting it quickly under control before throwing it 'like an arrow' to a swift-breaking winger. Possession, however, can be obtained by any defensive player through blocked shots, rebounds, fouls or intercepted passes. Occasionally more than one player is involved in the break and the ball is moved rapidly up the court by players interpassing at close range and at speed.

The classical fast break has seven stages which may be illustrated thus (see figure 67):

Figure 67

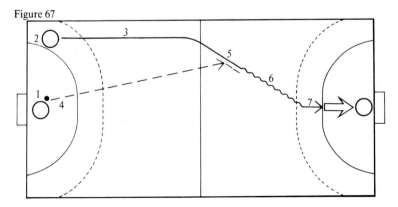

1  Keeper secures control of the ball
2  Speed off the mark by the breaking winger
3  Direction and speed of winger's route
4  Long accurate throw from the keeper
5  Catching of the throw at speed by the winger
6  Control of the ball by the winger using his maximum permitted number of steps and/or dribbling
7  Conclusion of the movement with an accurate shot

The winger should, in fact, score every time with a shot of his choice, usually the 6 metre jump shot or running shoulder shot. A lob would be used if he observed that the keeper had come too far off his line.

### Extended fast break

As the name suggests, this second phase of attacking play is an extension of the fast break. Throughout the fast break the ball movement is continuously towards goal at speed, whereas in the extended break the ball moves forward quickly in the initial stages but its progress is then slightly delayed. The attackers use lateral movements, probing out a gap in the rapidly regrouping defence or an overlap on the wings to exploit in, for example, a two-against-one situation. A number of fast accurate passes are strung together as other attackers arrive in support. If a shot cannot be fired at goal before the six defenders are in position round the 6 metre line, then the attackers abandon the extended break and slow the game pace down concentrating on scoring using recognized systems of attack.

### Systems of attack

This phase develops when the attacking team faces a complete and organized defence whether as a result of normal play or as a breakdown of the extended break. The attackers then play the ball around in a variety of recognized attacking moves each designed to test the opposition's defence and to exploit its weaknesses. These systems are described and analysed in chapter 10.

### Set pieces

Play resumes in this manner following the award of a free throw for an offence or the ball going out of play. The resultant short break for the re-introduction of the ball into play allows both teams time to position their players in accordance with the given situation. There are two particularly important set pieces:

(i)  the 9 metre free throw
(ii)  the corner throw

In each case the attackers execute a carefully prearranged and practised move involving, hopefully, an element of surprise and an ability to improvise according to changing defensive circumstances. The 9 metre free throw affords more scoring opportunities than the corner throw (figures 77–84).

**Phases of defence**

The corresponding phases of defensive play are:

(i)  countering the fast and extended fast breaks by spoiling and delaying tactics
(ii)  organization of the defensive wall
(iii)  systems of defence

*Countering the fast break*

A team is on the defensive the moment they lose possession. Even before loss (or gain) of possession both teams are ever alert to their prospective sudden change of roles from defence to attack and vice versa. The most effective counterplay against the fast break demands the player or players nearest to those making the break to harass and delay as the other defenders retreat with the utmost speed. The first part of the defensive wall to regroup should be that round the 6 metre line directly in front of goal as this is the most vulnerable part of a team's defence. When this area has been secured width is added on the flanks. Retreating defenders must watch the ball as well as the movements and progress of attackers coming up in support.

*Organization*

With the fast and extended fast breaks successfully stalled there is still, however, a period of uncertainty and danger as defenders find themselves out of position round the 6 metre line; they may not be in their accustomed, trained and most effective defensive capacity. Their combined efficiency must be strengthened by switching around carefully – this reorganization requires restraint, timing and co-ordination.

## Systems of defence

Composure and relaxation return to the team when the players have returned to their normal positions. The attackers, sensing this, will then start to employ their own particular systems in an effort to beat the defence. The defence will counter in this tactical battle by selecting a system to combat the attackers; common defence systems are analysed and described in detail on pages 138–46.

### Fast break practices

Goals scored from fast breaks should be evaluated not only in terms of quantity but also of the time in the game at which they occur. Quite often a team under pressure, especially late in a match, can snatch crucial goals from these breaks. Each of the seven stages of the classical break can be practised in isolation or together. In general, however, there are at least four stages to fast break progressions: individual breaks; breaks in pairs; breaks in threes; and breaks in groups.

## Individual

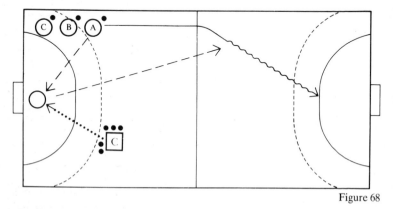

Figure 68

*Figure 68*: A passes to the keeper, sprints up the court, receives the keeper's throw and dribbles the ball to shoot from the 6 metre line.

B follows and so on. As an alternative the coach may set the move in motion by firing at the goalkeeper who then follows the course of action described.

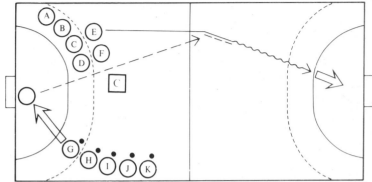

Figure 69

*Figure 69*: G shoots for the keeper to save. As he shoots the coach shouts the letter (E) of one of the players standing around the 6 and 9 metre lines. That player breaks, collects the keeper's throw, dribbles and shoots. Player H shoots and coach shouts another letter and so on.

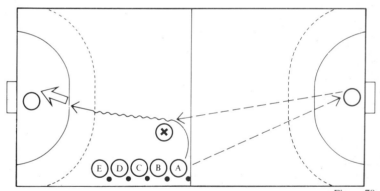

Figure 70

*Figure 70*: A throws the ball to the keeper and sprints round the marker to receive the return throw, dribbles and shoots past the opposition goalkeeper; B repeats.

### In pairs

*Figure 71*: A passes to the keeper. Both A and C break up court. C receives the keeper's throw and interpasses with A, either scoring at the other end. Players B and D repeat.

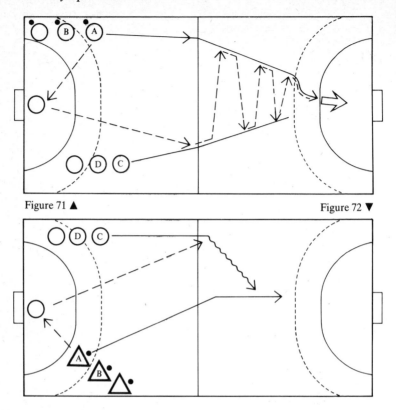

Figure 71 ▲                                        Figure 72 ▼

*Figure 72*: A passes to the goalkeeper and breaks as a retreating defender. C breaks as the attacker receiving the keeper's long throw and tries to score despite A's harassment. B and D repeat.

*In threes*

*Figure 73*: A passes to the keeper and all three (A,B,C) break. C receives the goalie's pass at speed and the three interpass up the court at speed with one shooting for goal. To make the task more realistic defenders D and E may be added to the court.

*In groups*

*Figure 74*: A throws the ball across court to B who is sprinting up for the pass. B catches the ball, dribbles and goes behind C's line. A then runs to the rear of B's line. C and D then do likewise at the other end.

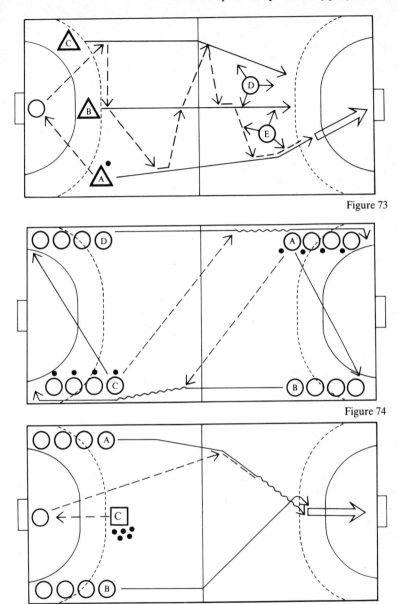

Figure 73

Figure 74

Figure 75

*Figure 75*: when the coach throws the ball at the keeper both front players (A and B) in each line sprint. The keeper decides to throw the ball to any one of the players who must try to score at the other end whilst the free player acts as a defender.

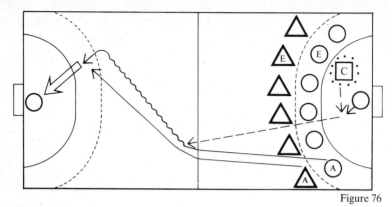

Figure 76

*Figure 76*: attackers line round the 9 metre line with a corresponding defender on the 6 metre line. Each pair is given a letter. The coach throws the ball to the keeper at the same time shouting a letter. The players whose letter has been called break and the goalkeeper throws to the attacker who has to attempt to score against the attentions of the defender. The coach may shout more than one letter at a time progressing to all the players being involved in the one break.

*Free throw set pieces*

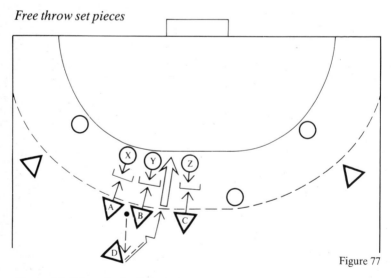

Figure 77

*Figure 77*: B has the ball and plays it to the big jump shooter D. A, B and C move forward to block the defenders X, Y and Z. The jump shooter shoots over the screen.

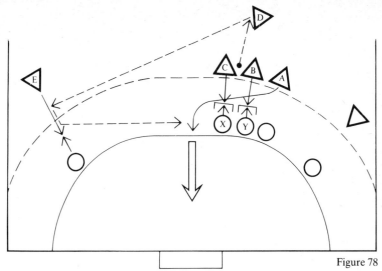

Figure 78

*Figure 78*: B has the ball, passes to D while B and C block defenders Y and X. D passes to E as he advances in. E passes to A who has come across behind the block.

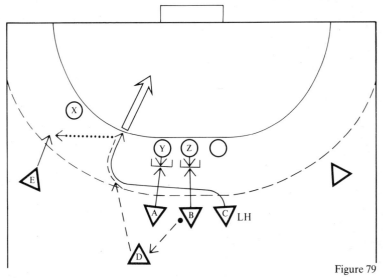

Figure 79

*Figure 79*: B has the ball and passes to D. A and B block defenders Y and Z. Left hander C moves across behind the block to receive pass from D, and (a) if unopposed shoots or (b) if defender X moves to cover then C passes to E who scores from the two-against-one situation.

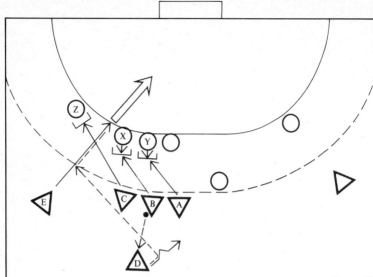

Figure 80

*Figure 80*: B passes to D. A and B block defenders Y and X. C blocks Z. D moves round and jump passes to E who is driving in for goal.

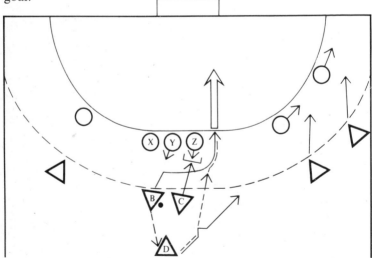

Figure 81

*Figure 81*: B passes to D. C blocks Z. B moves to block Y but swerves to the right behind C's block and receives D's jump pass to shoot.

*Corner throw set pieces*

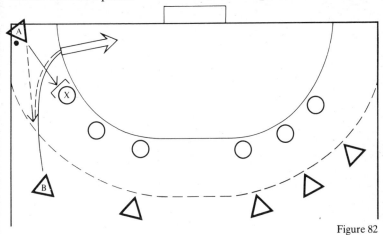

Figure 82

*Figure 82*: A passes to B and blocks defender X. B comes round wide, collects pass and shoots.

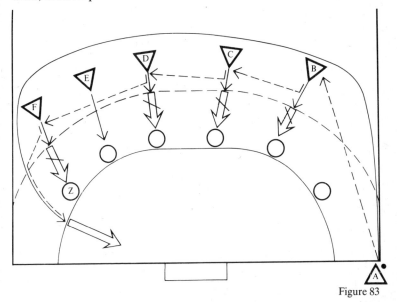

Figure 83

*Figure 83*: A passes to B, who fakes shot and passes to C, who fakes shot and passes to D, who fakes and passes to F, who drives in to shoot but, having committed defender Z, F releases the ball with a pass to A who has run the full circle.

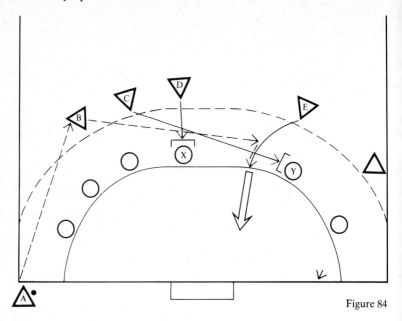

Figure 84

*Figure 84*: A passes to B, who passes to E, who is driving in. Defenders Y and X are blocked by C and D respectively.

# 9 Principles and practice of defence

The winning team in handball is, obviously, the one which concedes the least number of goals. Players adopt a defensive role immediately possession of the ball is lost. Individually and collectively they work to prevent goals being scored against them. The success of any defence depends on the quality of the players available, and their degree of tactical knowledge. The team's defence is only as strong as its weakest member, physically, mentally and tactically.

Teams must train in the defensive skills and techniques which, in combination with playing experience, will develop competence in tackling, containing opponents, working as a unit, anticipating tactical moves and 'reading' the opposition's attacks. Each individual must possess a set of wide-ranging defensive skills. Groups of defenders must co-ordinate to counter tactical moves and the team must perform as a fluid unit when operating selected defence systems. Vulnerable points of the defence must be protected through a concentration of resources and to do this the players must be equipped physically, psychologically and technically. The backs in the attack usually form the central core of the defence to give a solid foundation of height and strength.

## Individual defensive skills and techniques

Apart from the normal defensive qualities shared with other ball sports – anticipation, determination, mobility, speed of recovery, etc. – handball defenders require a number of characteristic qualities.

When possession is lost each player sprints back to the goal area keeping both the ball and the movement of the attackers under surveillance. The shortest route is the fastest unless spoiling and harassment is required as in the case of the fast breaks (pages 115–

Figure 85

16). When in position (figure 85) the correct defensive stance is adopted a balanced position, legs slightly flexed for rapid movement either forwards or backwards and, in preparation for possible jumping, feet about 30 centimetres apart, arms flexed out in front of the body ideally with the thumbs opposite the shoulders facing inwards in a 'W' position, the head held high and the eyes alert. Forward and reverse moves are made by short, rapid steps while lateral moves require a shuffling of the feet sideways (never cross the feet). Defenders must keep on the goal side of the attackers between ball and goal and must be able to block shots high, low and to the side. When blocking shots on the 9 metre line (figure 86) the defender advances out, meets the shooter with his body, and uses his hands to

Figure 86

block the ball. When advancing out defenders must ensure they are balanced to guard against attackers beating them in a one-on-one situation. Defenders must constantly talk to each other, indicate and signal players to be 'picked up' or covered. They must also anticipate passes, shots, blocks, crosses, screens and tactical moves played on them by attackers both individually and collectively. If an attacker gets behind a defender round the 6 metre line then that defender must 'feel' for the attacker without turning round. The collective defensive wall is illustrated in figure 87.

There are a number of specific, individual defensive techniques which require intensive training.

Figure 87

*Pressing and containing individual opponents*

It is important for defenders to be able to mark individual attackers closely. If the defender is 'ball watcher' the attacker who is being marked can often drift quite skilfully out of that defender's sight into open space. Two useful practices in defence training are:

Figure 88

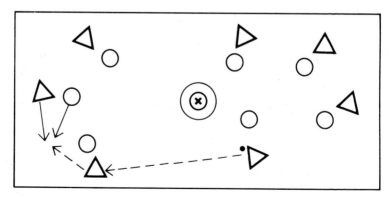

 (i) a game of handball with man-to-man marking all over the court
(ii) defending the marker (figure 88). A circle is chalked on the
    floor and a marker placed inside. Attackers with the ball play it
    around whilst defenders mark closely trying to intercept and
    dispossess. A goal is scored when an attacking player receives
    the ball and runs in with the ball to touch the marker without
    first being touched by his nominated defender, on the same
    lines as 'touch rugby'. If he is touched as he runs in then his
    team lose possession and the teams change round. Players must
    constantly be on the move, the three step rule is in force, and no
    one can enter the circle without the ball.

## Lines of movement

Defenders moving out to cover opponents driving in towards the
free throw line do not move forwards and backwards on the same
straight line. They move in an inverted 'V' path, the direction of
both forward and backward moves being influenced by the direction and movement of the ball.

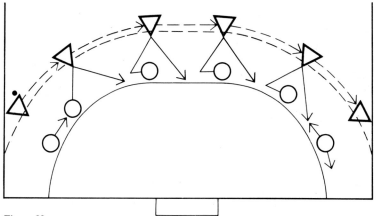

Figure 89

    Figure 89 relates to the movement of defenders in the 6–0 forma-
tion with the ball moving left to right. Both wingers move only
*laterally* while the four central defenders move *out and back diagon-*
*ally* to attack the ball holders and return to strengthen the defence
at the points of greatest vulnerability. A training practice for this
routine is indicated in figure 90.

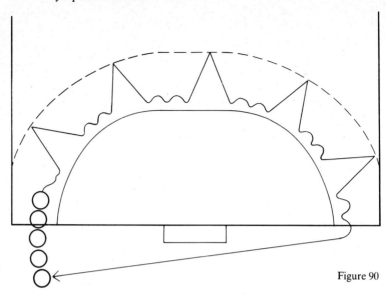

Figure 90

## Body checking

Defenders, within the framework of the rules, can move out to impede or obstruct the movement of circle runners to reduce their effectiveness and the fluidity of their attack. Figure 91 illustrates a training practice for this skill.

Figure 91

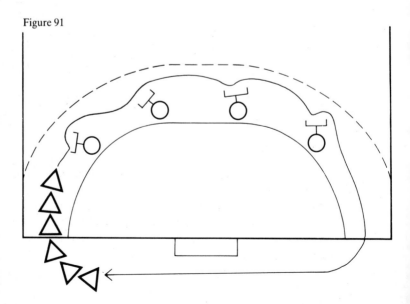

## Dispossession and blocking shots

*Dispossession*: players train to be able to dispossess attackers in the act of shooting. The aim is to steal or remove the ball cleanly from the shooter's hand from all positions whether in front, to the side, behind or in the air. This, of course, must be accomplished legitimately, unlike the foul on the shooter shown in figure 92.

Figure 92

*Blocking shots*: once the ball has left the shooter's hand defenders must be able to block its progress to goal. Half-hearted efforts can often result in deflections past the helpless keeper. Shots must be blocked high, low, to the side, etc. Blocking practices for defenders against lines of attackers are (figure 93):

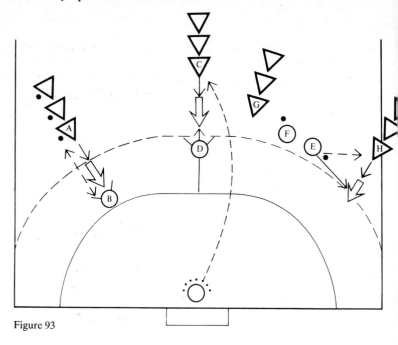

Figure 93

(i)  A passes to B, receives return and shoots with B blocking
(ii)  Keeper passes to C who advances and shoots. D moves to block
(iii)  E passes to H who advances to 9 metre line to shoot. E moves across to block. F and G do likewise

## Winning possession of fifty-fifty balls

Possession in handball is all-important, and players must be trained to win fifty–fifty balls from, for example, rebounds from the goals and blocked shots, etc.

Players in teams A and B (figure 94) scatter round the sports hall. The coach stands about 4 metres from one player in the B team, to whom he bounces the ball. That player fists the ball down the hall and members of both teams move to secure possession. After twenty hits the teams change round and a record is kept of the score.

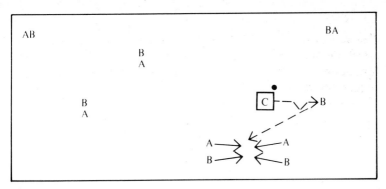

Figure 94

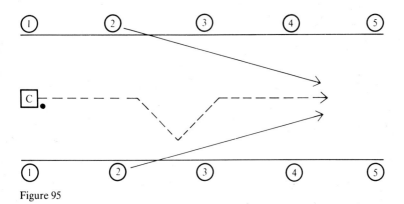

Figure 95

Another practice is shown in figure 95. Two lines of players, each with a number, lie motionless on their backs, feet facing inwards. The coach shouts a number and bounces the ball along a midway line. Those whose number has been called get up as fast as they can and sprint after the ball to gain possession. Again a score is kept for each team.

### Group defensive skills and techniques

Defensive systems require, as far as possible, *width, depth* and *density*. To satisfy these requirements players have to work collectively through a number of skills, practices and techniques.

*Falling out*

This occurs when one defender moves out to the 9 metre line to attack the ball holder and then returns to strengthen the defence formation. As a player falls out colleagues move across to cover (figures 96 and 97).

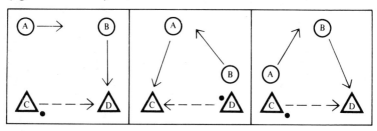

Figure 96 ▲                                                    Figure 97 ▼

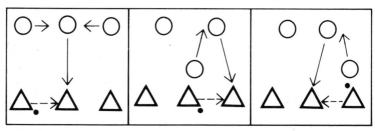

  (i) C passes to D. Defender B moves out to cover the ball holder. Defender A moves across to reinforce at this point of potential vulnerability
 (ii) D passes back to C and A moves out diagonally to cover the ball holder. B retreats in a similar path to secure the defence behind A
(iii) C passes to D who is picked up by B with A retreating to cover penetration behind B

*This skill of 'falling out' is absolutely fundamental to defensive play in handball.*

The falling-out technique forms the basis of the 6–0 defence.

*Receive, escort and handover*

In a two-against-two situation when two attackers switch positions each defender covers the movement of his attacker and then takes

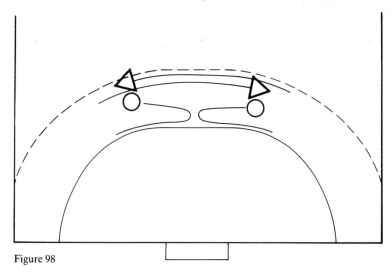

Figure 98

over the marking of the next player as the switch is made. This skill, illustrated in figure 98, is frequently used to cover the movement of circle runners. Simple practices can be easily devised by the coach involving all players.

*Support*

Players must at all times co-operate with their colleagues, giving assistance when necessary. Figure 87 shows a solid unified defensive wall. Apart from the obvious support required for falling out, this aspect of defence is vital for.

(i)   *blocking shots* – two defenders, for example, in the 5–1 system can be very effective *together*

(ii)  *countering blocks* – defenders train to anticipate blocks and to neutralize these and other such tactical moves.

(iii) *overlap situations* – defenders must learn how to cope with both the extra man and the man short

*Doubling up*

Team members occasionally double up to guard a particularly dangerous ball holder or to prevent penetration. This is only temporary and should be used with discretion.

**Defensive systems**

The most successful and widely used defence systems in handball
are *zone* defences in which each defender is responsible for an area
relative to his team-mates (as in basketball). Therefore any attacker who 'invades' the zone must be covered. The actual location of
the zone changes as the defence moves laterally following the movement of the ball. There are four popular systems – the 6–0 and 5–1
are equally popular and are used in over 80 per cent of play in top-
class handball with the 4–2 and 3–2–1 formations being employed
much less frequently.

| | | Defence system | | | |
|---|---|---|---|---|---|
| *Positions of players* | | 6 – 0 | 5 – 1 | 4 – 2 | 3 – 2 – 1 |
| wingers | left wing | × | × | × | × |
| | right wing | × | × | × | × |
| half-backs | left half-back | × | × | × | |
| | right half-back | × | × | × | |
| backs | left back | × | | | |
| | centre back | | × | | × |
| | right back | × | | | |
| forwards | left forward | | | × | × |
| | centre forward | | × | | × |
| | right forward | | | × | × |

Figure 99 (above) explains the names and positions of the defenders for these systems.

*The 6–0 system*

In the 6–0 system all the defenders position themselves on the
6 metre line (Figures 100–102), giving good width. Although depth
is lacking this is achieved at points of potential vulnerability by the
'falling out' technique which is employed by the four central defenders, the wingers confining themselves to lateral movement
only. In a 6–0 defence each defender is responsible for an opponent
in a 'counting-off' system.

Figure 103 shows this counting-off system in operation against a
3–3 attack. The defence divides into two groups, left and right, and,
commencing from the wings, count off to three. In the operation of

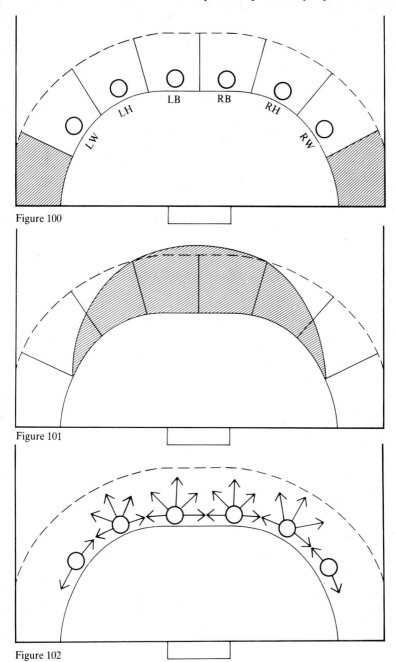

Figure 100

Figure 101

Figure 102

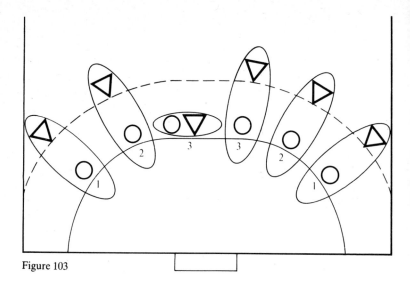

Figure 103

this system group skills are important especially covering, falling out and escorting players. The 6–0 is vulnerable to good distant shooters and active wing play. The 2–4 attack with two mobile pivots positioned wide creates danger. Attacking teams are permitted time to organize their tactical moves, possession is sometimes unchallenged and fast breaks are difficult to come by. However, as it incorporates many sound defensive skills it is the best system to introduce to learners.

Figure 104 features the 6–0 defence against a 2–4 attack.

### The 5–1 system

In this system five defenders are positioned round the goal area line with the sixth a chaser out in front (figures 105–107). This last player tries to contain the initial attacks, intercept passes, initiate fast breaks and generally harass attacking backs. The 5–1, however, is weakish on width, requiring instant covering from team-mates when danger threatens. The deployment of the defenders in this central core area is vital to this particular defence. The centre back goes laterally to cover for the halves who are constantly falling out to attack the ball holder. Figure 108 shows the 5–1 defence in operation against a 3–3 attack.

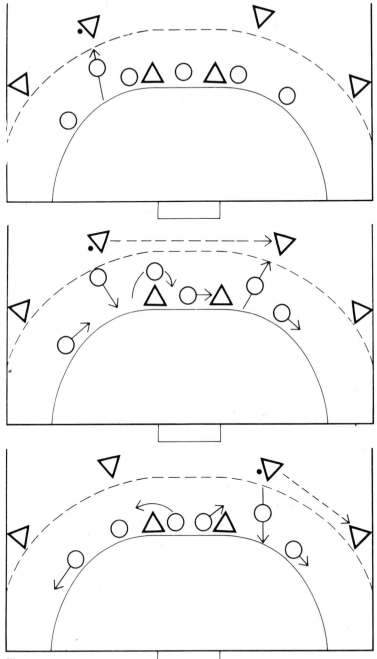

Figure 104

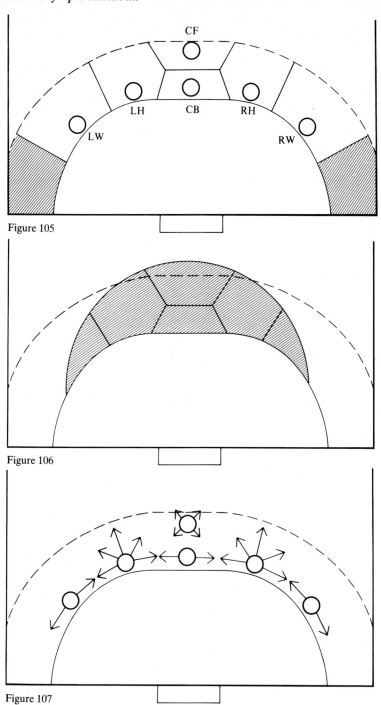

Figure 105

Figure 106

Figure 107

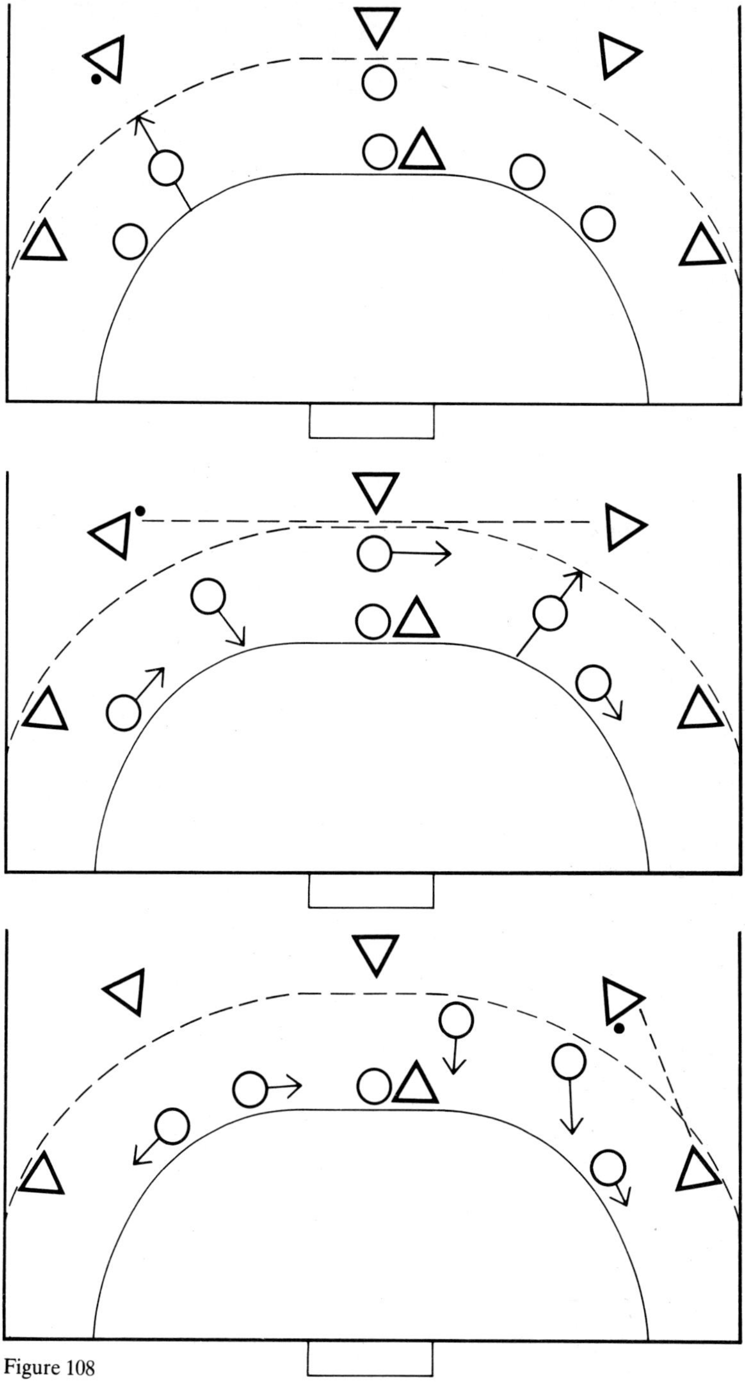

Figure 108

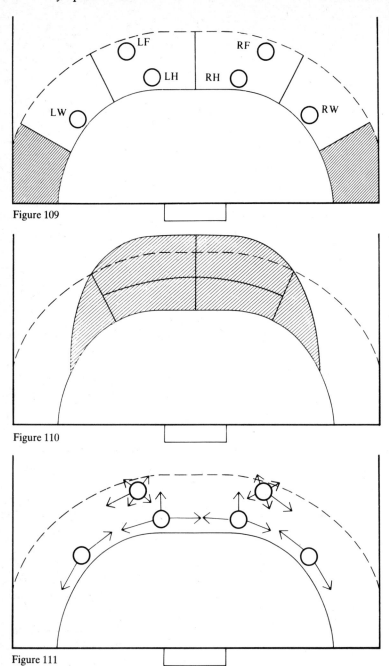

Figure 109

Figure 110

Figure 111

The 5–1 system is vulnerable to active wing play and to distant shooting when the chaser is taken out of the game by screens and blocks. Good pivot play and a concentration of attack on the central core create weaknesses.

## The 4–2 system

Two forwards are positioned out in front of the defence to look for interceptions, stop distant shooters and initiate fast-breaks. The defence has depth but lacks width and is susceptible to fast-moving play and skilful elusive wingers who find time and space to advantage. Figures 109, 110 and 111 illustrate the basis of this defensive system. Figure 112 features part of its movement against a 2–4 attack.

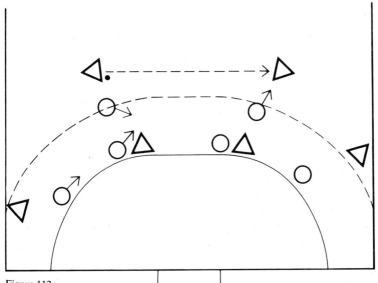

Figure 112

## 3–2–1 defence

In terms of goals conceded this system is, perhaps, the most secure. All the defenders concentrate on the player in possession of the ball and the system has density and depth (figure 113) but is lacking in width with obvious resultant weaknesses. It is susceptible to line and wing play especially against a two-pivot attack. It is strong against distant shooters and good for fast breaks.

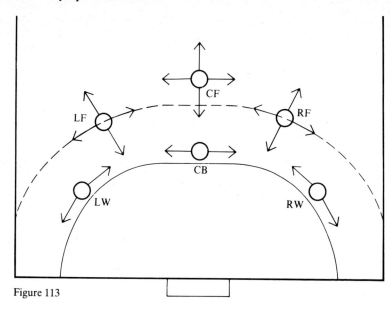

Figure 113

Figure 114 explains how this system operates against a 3–3 attack with a moving pivot.

*Man-to-man defence*

This is used in special circumstances such as pressurizing a team with one player short or to increase the tempo of the game in the closing stages when the scores are close. Each defender is responsible for an opponent who is followed and pressurized (into mistakes hopefully) round the court.

**Set pieces**

The important set pieces include the free throw, the corner throw and the penalty throw.

*Free throw* (see also page 21)

The direct line of the shot is usually blocked by three tall defenders while the remainder cover the attackers especially those who are possibilities for receipt of the first pass (figure 115).

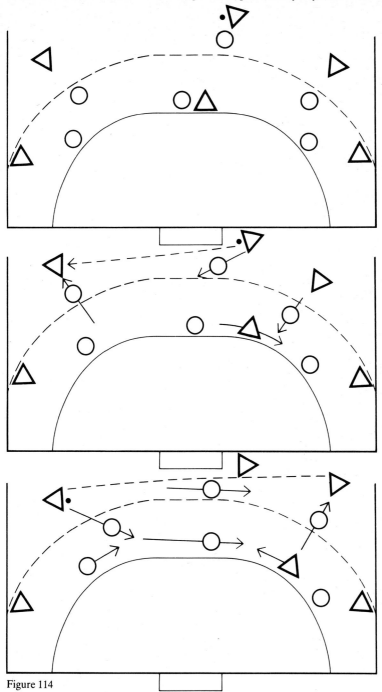

Figure 114

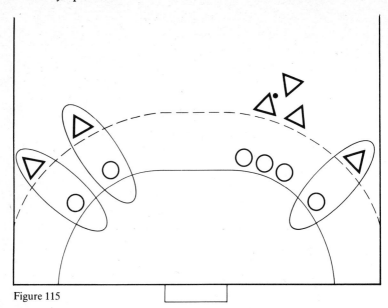

Figure 115

*Corner throw* (see also page 21)

Here each defender (figure 116) simply aligns himself with an attacker.

Figure 116

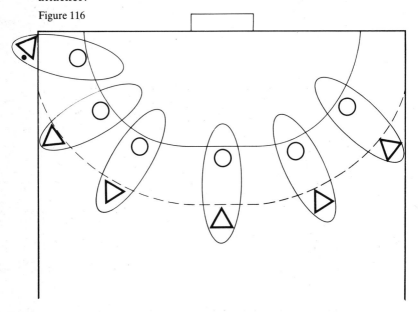

Figure 117

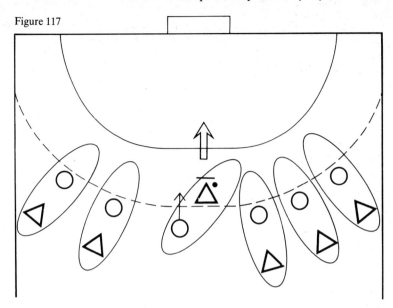

*Penalty throw* (see also page 22)

Defences usually line up in the best possible formation for dealing with rebounds (figure 117).

# 10 Principles and practice of attack

Handball is a comparatively high-scoring game which revolves round intense play in front of both goals. Unlike soccer there is no midfield contest; this part of the court is vacated primarily by the team on the defensive who retreat at speed to guard their goal the moment possession is lost.

In top-class handball a goal is scored in about 35 per cent of attacks mounted. Unlike soccer, again, this is relatively high and is important for three reasons.

The maintenance of possession is the foundation of successful attacking play as it allows players to manoeuvre for the best shooting positions amid diversionary movements and split-second changes in action. The court area in front of the defence is the scene of fast, dynamic action; one mistimed pass or misunderstanding amongst attackers and the whole movement breaks down.

When in a good shooting situation a player must be successful with his positioning, preparation and delivery. Players only shoot if they know from training and experience that their chances of scoring are high.

The qualities related to possession and shooting come only from a balanced and disciplined team; handball squads cannot go out to play without tactics nor can they rely solely on the effectiveness and genius of one or two players of exceptional talent. Handball is truly a team sport in which all the players display their basic skills and a high degree of tactical knowledge. The handball player must be equally skilled in attack and defence. The team must have full interchangeability with multi-purpose players within a mobile squad.

A certain psychological attitude is needed. The development of a handball *team* comes from the comprehensive training of players based on sound scientific analysis and methodology, an increase in the pace of the game and a thirst for victory displayed in a tenacious offensive spirit. Manoeuvres can be executed so forcefully that more tactically sophisticated teams collapse under the pressure in 60 minutes of solid action. A successful team has an appetite for self-expression and self-affirmation and will triumph through technical perfection and the will to win.

The object of each attack is to score a goal. All the players in a team involve themselves in tactical moves devised to create a two-against-one situation. Shooters must anticipate, react and shoot instantaneously when an often momentary overlap appears. Such openings are created from a combination of fast, rapid passing and the intelligent positioning and movement of players combined with individual and group attacking skills and techniques. At all times during an attacking strategy the ball holder commits a defender while others, individually or collectively, work on a manoeuvre to confuse the operation of a specific defender or group of defenders. Attack is best analysed under three headings: individual attack; group attack; and attacking systems.

## Individual attack

Individual attacking techniques are the basis of group and team strategies.

### Stance

The attacker stands in a balanced position with one foot ahead of the other ready for movement. His hands and arms face the ball while his head is held high and eyes alert watching movements of defenders, attackers and the ball.

### Movement

The attacker must be fast off his mark, be able to accelerate, stop, start, turn and move powerfully in short abrupt and explosive lines of action.

### Positioning

Throughout passing movements and player exchanges attackers must position themselves in open spaces offering themselves as passing possibilities constantly increasing the team's number of options.

*Running into contact zones*

Players driving for goal with or without the ball threaten the contact zone between defenders to maximize the possibility of penetration resulting from the confusion created by two defenders moving simultaneously to cover the danger. Figures 118 and 119 illustrate such lines of movement against the 6–0 and 5–1 defensive systems.

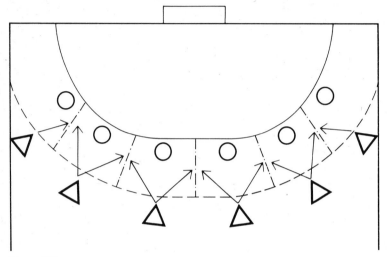

Figure 118

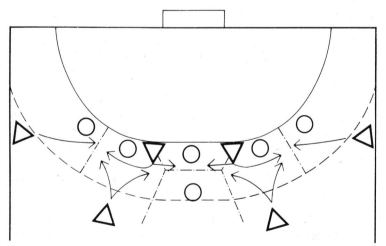

Figure 119

*Creating space round the 6 metre line*

Players operating temporarily or permanently round the 6 metre line manoeuvre themselves round to the 'wrong side' of a defender so that right handers have defenders on their left side when they are facing goal. On receipt of a pass or 'feed' the ball is shielded from the defender reducing the chances of dispossession during shooting. Figure 120 illustrates the movements of the line players round the 6 metre line seeking out space.

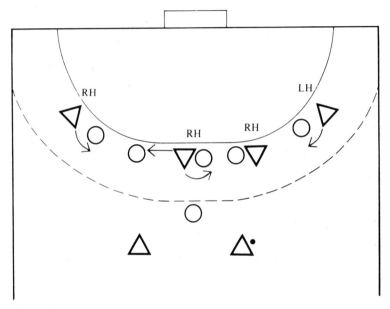

Figure 120

*Committing defenders*

One of the first attacking skills to be learned is the possible lines of movement open to the ball holder, who must at all times during an attacking move commit and pressurize a defender so that the particular defender cannot contribute to the neutralizing of the attacking team's next move. The defence, therefore is stretched at all times. Teams usually line up in the 6–0 or 5–1 defensive systems (pages 138–143). Possible lines of movement against such systems are illustrated in figures 121 and 122.

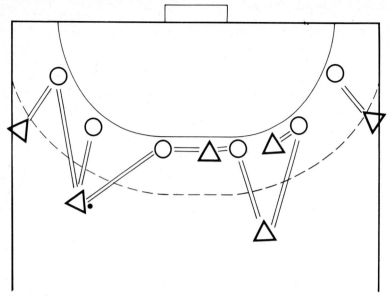

Figure 121

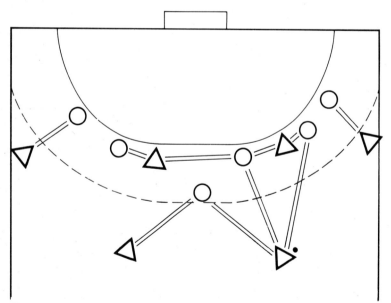

Figure 122

*Beating defenders in a one-versus-one situation*

A player driving in on goal can create scoring opportunities by beating and going past his covering defender. If another defender moves across to cover this danger then the defence is weakened as the possibilities for an overlap are created (provided, of course, team mates have moved quickly in support). Each attacker in turn commits a defender until the extra player is released to shoot unopposed. There are at least four methods where an attacker can beat his opposite number although in top-class handball the super-tight defences are not so easily prised open.

*Swerve*

A swerve is often used by the big shooters in the back division as they drive in towards goal. The footwork is so arranged that the foot determining the direction of the swerve is in front. On contact with the floor thrust is given in the desired direction. Right handers usually push off the left foot towards the right (figure 123). Players must remember to adhere to the three step rule.

Figure 123

Figure 124

### *Turns* (figure 124)

Turns are characteristic of wingers and line players and are particularly effective against immobile defenders. The attacker commits a defender by moving in to shoot. Instead of shooting, the player pivots on his left foot spinning round anti-clockwise holding the ball centrally to increase the speed of the turn and to maintain close ball control. As he comes out of the turn he pushes off the pivoting foot (which is the left for right handers) and times his movement past the often hesitant or unbalanced defender. Line players must be able to turn equally effectively in both directions.

### *Sidestep*

This short sideways movement (as in rugby football for instance) is much less common.

### *Feint or dummy*

The attacker moves forward and completes the action (not the delivery!) for a pass or shot but at the exact moment of release brings the ball back under control and commences another movement.

In the first three manoeuvres above, the attacker runs at the defender and begins his actions at a point just in front of the defender. He looks at him or in the direction in which he wants the defender to think he is going employing a slight deceleration to prepare the legs for the thrust and subsequent burst of speed to follow.

**Group attack**

There are a number of skills and techniques involving two or more players which, when trained and executed, will produce the maximum amount of positive play within an overall attacking system. These group skills are first learned in isolation then practised in improvised matches. Constant training is needed to improve versatility, timing and co-ordination.

*Double pass*

This 'double' or 'return' pass (as in the 'wall' pass in soccer) allows a player to be released to drive in for goal unopposed, for example, a back passing to a pivot and sprinting on to shoot on receipt of the return pass (figure 125). Simple practices for this can easily be devised.

Figure 125

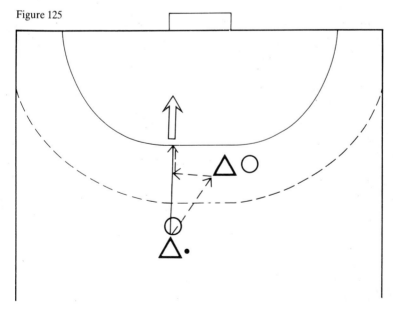

*Parallel pass*

This parallel or side pass is a recognized method of moving the ball along a line of attackers when an overlap presents itself or when attackers are manoeuvring to beat defenders. Two attackers can, for instance, outwit two defenders by employing a swerve, and a drive into the contact zone culminating in a final parallel pass into the clear (figure 126).

Figure 126

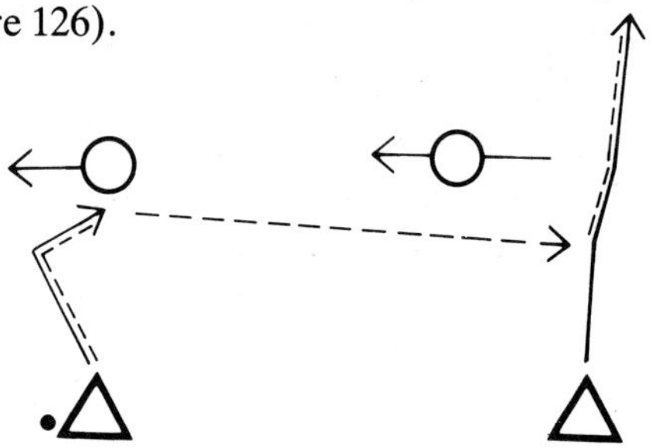

This practice can be equally effective in the three-against-two, four-against-three, five-against-four, or six-against-five situation where the defenders are drawn across out of position and the overlap created for the extra man.

*Crossing*

This is a widely used manoeuvre to confuse defenders and create scoring chances. Players may cross with or without the ball (again,

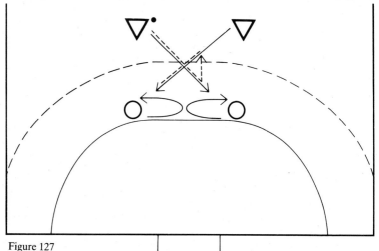

Figure 127

as an example from another sport – the dummy scissors in rugby football). Those involved in crossing pass close to each other and the ball holder slips the ball to his colleague using sometimes a concealed pass. The correct countermeasure for defenders is to 'turn back' to cover the crossing player as in figure 127, which illustrates a simple crossing move, with countermeasures. Once more, simple practices are easily devised involving two lines of players.

*Screening*

This movement is similar to crossing. The aim is for one player to move in front of a defender to obstruct not only his movement but also his view of the ball holder whom that particular defender is covering. The defender and sometimes the keeper are temporarily unsighted thereby greatly diminishing their capability of reaction to a sudden snap shot. Screens are common in set pieces such as 9 metre free throws (as illustrated on pages 122–124).

*Blocking and freeing*

Blocking occurs when an attacker places his body in front of a defender to restrict his desired line of defensive movement. A well-timed block will give a second attacker time and space to shoot or engage in a further move.

Figure 128                                                    Figure 129

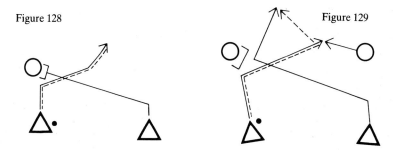

Blocking in a two-against-one situation is illustrated in figure 128.

Blocking in a two-against-two situation is rendered more effective when the player making the block releases (or frees) himself quickly into play to receive a pass, often a concealed pass (figure 129). Blocking techniques require long and careful practice.

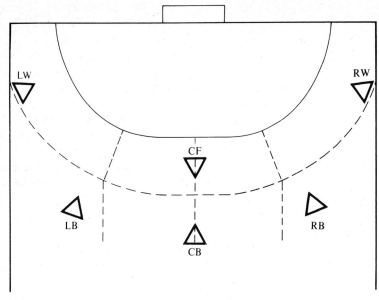

Figure 130

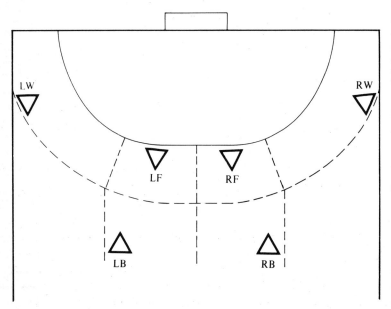

Figure 131

## Attacking systems

The positioning of the players of the offensive team determines the formation and the name of the possible systems of attack in handball. The choice of formation depends on the capabilities of the attackers and on the defensive tactics of the opponents. The most common attacking systems are:

3–3 (one line player)

2–4 (two line players)

The composition of both these systems and the positions of the players on the court are self-explanatory (figures 130, 131 and 132).

|  |  | Attack system | |
| --- | --- | :---: | :---: |
| *Position of players* |  | 2 – 4 | 3 – 3 |
| wingers | left wing | × | × |
|  | right wing | × | × |
| backs | left back | × | × |
|  | centre back |  | × |
|  | right back | × | × |
| forwards | left forward | × |  |
|  | centre forward |  | × |
|  | right forward | × |  |

Figure 132

## Qualities of the attacking players

In attack there are players in three distinct positions each with individual characteristics:

Backs
Wingers
Forwards (known as circle or line players or, perhaps, more aptly
    described as target men or pivots)

### Backs

The backs are the heart and brains of the team's attack and operate in the 'engine room' (like midfield soccer players). They are usually

tall, commanding, physically strong, confident, skilful and dominant being superbly equipped physically, mentally and technically.
They have a thorough knowledge of the principles of play and are
masters of passing, ball control and shooting. Their authority is
stamped on the game through skill, fitness, creativity, artistry,
strength and the ability for instant communication with other members of their team. Briefly, the backs must be able to drive forward,
run at defenders, beat opponents in a one-against-one situation,
combine in manoeuvres with team-mates and be able to shoot accurately and powerfully. Psychologically they must have an overbear-
ing desire to win and must want to be 'involved', demanding the
ball, controlling it and using it productively.

## Wingers

The main function of these fast, fit, elusive players is to bring width
to the attack, commit defenders and to create time and space for the
big shooters in the back division. Without effective wingers fluent
handball is highly unlikely. Wingers must have the ability to beat
their opposite number by making space on the flanks or by body
movements calling for speed, acceleration, balance, close control
and confidence. They should be versatile and inventive and have
the shooting accuracy to score from what is very often the narrowest
of angles.

## Line players

Much of a team's attacking strategy utilizes these tough, strong
target men. Their main function is to assist in the setting up of scoring chances for the backs as well as being able to put the ball in the
net themselves. Their function, therefore, calls for the ability and
courage to make room and offer themselves as passing possibilities
deep in the opposition's defence. They continually adjust their position in relation to the movement of the ball and of the defenders in
areas where space is usually restricted. They control the ball under
severe and physical challenges, rely heavily on the support of their
colleagues and run into positions even if the odds of positive results
are sometimes against such a movement. These line players require
special understanding as they display qualities requiring timing, co-
ordination, opportunism and confidence. An ability to *read* weaknesses in the defence and to *exploit* them develops through hard,

bruising training under match conditions. Nowadays big, strong, active, intelligent line players are replacing the smaller, more elusive type traditionally seen in the past.

*Physical and anatomical properties of international players*

Many of the leading handball nations have now begun to introduce taller and bigger players and this has in a number of instances injected too a high degree of aggression and rough play to counteract for the lack of athleticism and technique. The height of the average handball player in the last decade has gone up 3 centimetres to 187.5 centimetres (6 feet 1¾ inches) and has been accompanied by a 3 kilogram (6.5 pounds) increase in weight to 88 kilogram (13 stone 12 pounds). The smallest players are the pivots with a average height of 183 centimetres and weight of 83 kilogram (13 stone).

The arm span of players varies from 188 centimetres (6 feet 2 inches) for the pivots through to around 202 centimetres (6 feet 7½ inches) for the big shooting specialists in the back division, while the span of the hands for most players is about 24 centimetres (9½ inches). Indeed some countries have anatomical norms which are used as a criteria for selecting league and national teams. Cardiovascular tests on players show that they have the same efficiency as middle-distance track athletes and an average bodyweight oxygen consumption of around 70 millilitres per kilogram bodyweight. The motor activities involved in attacking play are also similar to track and field and are based on running, jumping and throwing. Handball players train to sprint 30 metres in around 3.8 seconds. The motor activities required for defence are more closely connected to gymnastic techniques. International teams often have up to eight specialists with them to advise and prepare the players for the major matches.

**Movement of the ball in attacking systems**

The ball is passed accurately and rapidly amongst the players in a series of short, well-executed ploys. The purpose is to switch the ball around at speed to pressurize the defence at all times with thrusts and lateral stretches to allow penetration at the centre and to pull out the heart of the defensive wall to prise space for the line players to operate. Figures 133 and 134 illustrate the possible lines of movement in the 2–4 and 3–3 attacking systems.

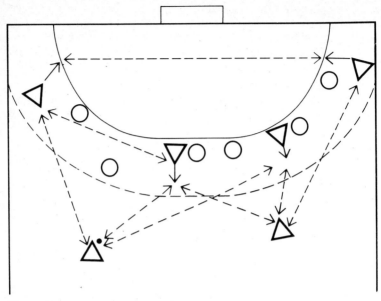

Figure 133

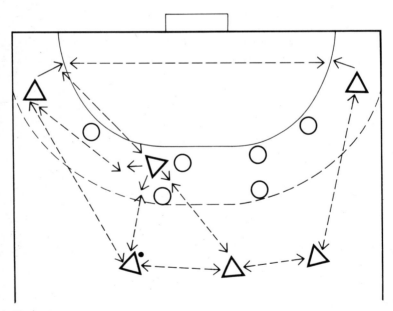

Figure 134

*Movement of players*

When the concept of ball movement has been acquired players will then learn how they themselves can move as a co-ordinated unit to increase their attacking potential. Tactical moves will be learned, practised and used in game situations. In a match players will position themselves in a pre-selected formation and then commence to move the ball round a recognized flight path. A signal will be given and players will move and interchange in tactical ploys either in groups of two, three four, five or all together. Using blocks, screens, crossing and other group and individual attacking techniques they attempt to disrupt the defence to gain penetration and create scoring chances. At all times during the movement of the players the key back positions must be filled. A simple training practice is shown in figure 135 (others can easily be devised and applied as required):

A passes to B, runs round circle, receives return pass, carries the
    ball, passes to C and joins end of line.
C passes to B, etc.

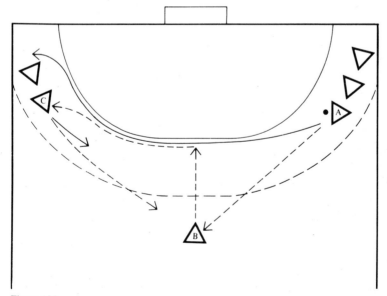

Figure 135

*Figure of eight*

Another common running pattern involving all the players in continuous movement is the 'figure of eight', a simple move (figure
136) where it is played by a 2–4 attack against a 5–1 defence.

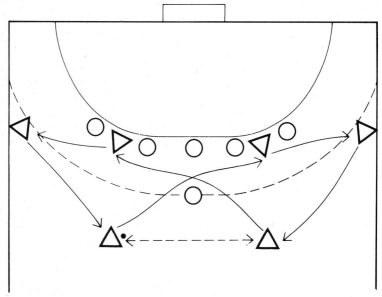

Figure 136

*Overlap situation*

Owing to injury or suspension a team may be temporarily reduced
to five players for a short period of time. The overlap must then be
ruthlessly exploited. Figure 137, illustrates one method where all
the attackers retreat outside the free throw line and play the ball
round with each player committing a defender in turn until the extra
man is released in a clear position.

This tactical move must be played at great speed because any
intelligent handicapped team will be aware that this move is likely
to be used against them and will move cover defence very quickly
from one side of the court to the other to reinforce the possible lines
of weakness. Figure 138 illustrates a 6 versus 5 overlap with one
pivot. Here one player on the six-metre line employs a block to
upset lateral covering movement of the defenders.

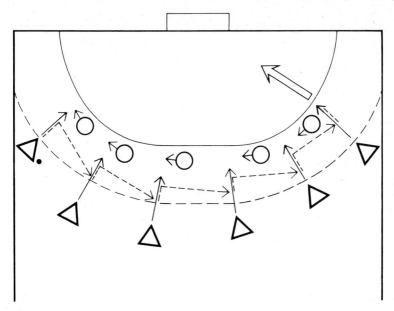

Figure 137

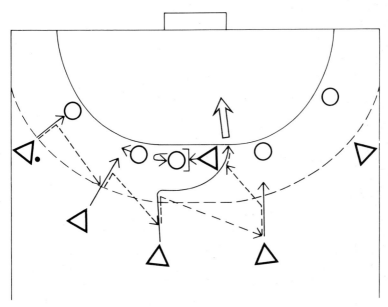

Figure 138

# 11 Conditioning and training

As with all sportsmen the handball player must be fully conditioned before he can even contemplate any specialized training relevant to his own particular requirements.

The true enthusiast will, of course, keep himself in condition all the year round, yet merely keeping fit is insufficient for the demands of playing regularly and competitively. In handball training the basic components of all-round physical preparedness must be considered right from the outset, namely – stamina, strength, suppleness, speed and skill.

**Stamina**

Stamina is best acquired through cross-country work, beginning approximately two months before the season starts. This the player may do, in the early stages, for two or three days a week. Initially the runs should be easy stepping up the pace as fitness improves. Keep the distances sensible – for example, it is better to run 2 to 3 miles fast or steadily than plod laboriously (and uncomfortably) for 8 or 9 miles. One of the beauties of cross-country is the change of scenery from the gym and indoor hall and also the opportunity it affords for running not only at various distances but also at varying pace such as in Fartlek training. This Swedish word means 'speed play' and may involve alternate bursts of hard and fast running with easier recovery periods. For instance a session of this kind may take the form of:

1 mile steady running
200–300 metre fast stride
½ mile jog
a couple of hill runs
¼ mile walk
2 mile steady

It is obvious that a whole variety of permutations can be used in this type of running. Roads may also be used but in view of the hard surfaces to be encountered in the months to come grass is much better at this stage.

## Strength

This is best acquired through circuit and weight training, especially the latter, once or, preferably, twice a week with special emphasis on exercises designed to improve the strength of muscles and joints most prominently featured in the game, i.e. half-squats, jump squats, split snatch, triceps stretch, wrist rolling, bench press, etc. Without detailing a sample programme it is sufficient to say that any proficient handball coach will soon assess the needs of the player in question and provide a suitable schedule as necessary. One important point about weight training – it must be *progressive*. Keep a record of the poundages used and note the improvement in the loads being used but, at the same time, never rush things. If gymnasium equipment is available to club or player, circuit training is another good way of improving strength. Circuits rarely last more than 15 minutes or so (because of their particularly 'sapping' nature) and are best used as an opening activity prior to, say, some technique, tactical or skill work. A list of exercises which might be used could include (figure 139):

(i) *press-ups from the finger tips* – this is particularly effective if the feet are elevated on a bench or in the wallbars
(ii) *back extension* – lie face downwards with the midriff across a bench and the feet anchored under the wallbars to the rear. Allow the head and shoulders to rest on a mat in front. Raise and lower the trunk alternately trying to obtain as great an arch in the back as possible
(iii) *squat thrusts to wallbars* – adopt a full squat position just in front of the wallbars grasping the bars with both hands slightly above head height. From there thrust vigorously upwards striking the wallbars with the chest as high as you possibly can. Repeat explosively till the required number of reps are completed
(iv) *wrist rolling* – attach one of the weight discs using a strong cord to either a dumb-bell bar or a thick piece of wood (length of cord should be approximately distance from hip height to floor) Simply wind the disc up by rotating the wrists until it is

Figure 139

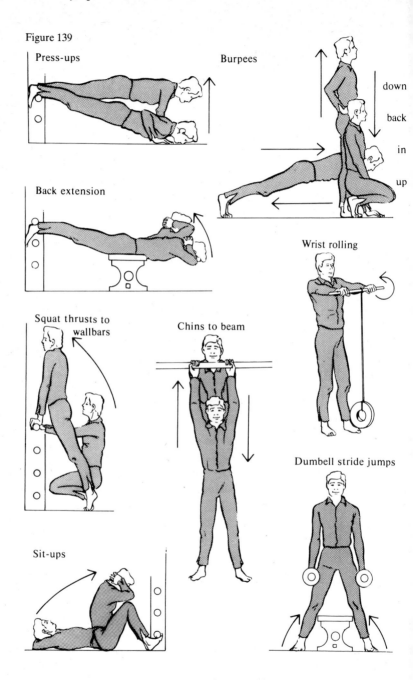

Press-ups

Burpees

down

back

in

up

Back extension

Wrist rolling

Squat thrusts to wallbars

Chins to beam

Dumbell stride jumps

Sit-ups

touching the bar then let it unwind down to floor again (and so on)

 (v) *sit ups* – lie on mat, hook feet under bench or wallbars and raise the body to the vertical after which it returns to the mat once more. Repeat as required

 (vi) *stride jumps* – stand astride a bench, a dumb-bell of appropriate weight in each hand. Jump up on to the top of the bench then down to the starting position alternately

(vii) *chins to the beam* – have the beam well above head height so that you have to jump off the floor to grasp it (*overgrasp* not *undergrasp!*). Raise the trunk till the *chin* clears the beam then extend the arms *fully* before repeating. Try to keep the body still, and fully extended, during upward and downward movements

(viii) *burpees* – start from the standing position. Squat down into the 'bunny' stance with the hands flat on the floor between the feet. Thrust the legs into full extension backwards, return to the squat position then stand up once more. Each return to the standing position counts as one repetition

There are, of course, a great many more exercises which the player may wish to utilize and these are entirely up to his own discretion and preference. Through experience he will soon discover what type of exercises/session is best suited to his needs. Weights may also be used in circuit training but since speed is so often the essence of this type of workout great care must be taken not only in terms of the type of exercise involved but in the *weight* involved.

The metal spring wrist exerciser or a sponge rubber ball is a useful pocket companion for handball players where constant squeezing helps to develop forearm muscles. Another useful contraption is a set of chest expanders (or similar pulley-type device) hooked to a wall, door, gatepost etc. from which the player can practise the throwing action against the resistance of the springs.

**Suppleness**

Suppleness is essential to the handball player, not just from the point of view of his own personal performance but also in helping to reduce the risk of injury. Suppling exercises should never be neglected and should be practised at home all the year round on a daily basis. A number of specific exercises have already been listed in the appropriate chapters and suitable stretching movements are included in the next chapter on injury prevention.

## Speed

For speed off the mark and full and intelligent exploitation of open space games such as touch rugby, indoor soccer, badminton and table tennis are useful. For a combination of speed and suppleness gymnastics (carefully supervised) can be of great benefit. The sprint coach of the local athletics club may be particularly helpful in the off-season period. A good exercise is to run at three-quarter speed for 100–150 yards down a track or soccer pitch accelerating every 10–15 yards or so into little short sprint bursts. The coach or his assistant can often help by blowing a whistle every so often as a signal to 'shoot forward'.

## Skill

Skill is acquired through experience and is improved through team practices as well as training for individual skills as listed in the appropriate chapters. Pre-season the handball player will obviously work to perfect his own particular requirements incorporating them into the team situation when early season team training commences.

So, a pre-season conditioning period might have:

*Day 1*  cross-country for stamina
*Day 2*  weight/circuit training
*Day 3*  rest
*Day 4*  cross-country
*Day 5*  weight training
*Day 6*  rest
*Day 7*  skill practices with the team

## Training sessions

From the comprehensive list of practices described in the previous chapters, the coach can devise simple or complex sessions as required.

# 12 Common injuries: treatment and prevention

Handball players, like any other sportsmen, are occasionally the victims of a 'freak' injury requiring hospital treatment which, in turn, sidelines the unfortunate recipient for a considerable time. Generally, however, handball injuries are as one might expect according to the nature of the game – sprained or 'staved' fingers and wrists, torn muscles and cartilage trouble in the knee joints, etc.

Perhaps the commonest site of injury is the fingers. Both in attack and in defence, as for example in 'blocking' the fingers run the risk of being 'bent back' and the joint capsules round these small, delicate joints are often torn with resultant pain and swelling. The cure for such an injury is simply rest, but this does not mean total inactivity for the entire hand. Only the finger (or fingers) concerned should be rendered inactive by being bound with tape to the nearest neighbouring finger (figure 140). The binding, you will notice, is *above* the actual joint itself. This is to prevent any uncomfortable restriction on the swelling which always occurs on injured

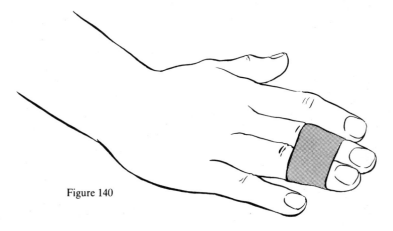

Figure 140

joints and also to allow for gentle re-introduction back to movement as the joint improves. Finely constructed joints are designed for constant active movement; that is why they should be encouraged back into action at the earliest opportunity (not too early!) and why only the finger concerned should be protected in the first instance. Strengthening of the fingers (and wrists) is important and players should do lots of exercises designed with this in mind – press-ups on finger tips, wrist rolling with weights, squeezing a rubber ball or metal wrist exerciser, etc.

Similar traumatic injuries as above occur in the wrist, more often through awkward falls than any blocking action. Again the joint must be immobilized but the fingers must always be kept active. An elastoplast strapping (applied in figure-of-eight fashion round wrist and hand leaving the thumb protruding) is ideal for protecting and supporting the joint during the recovery period. Strengthening exercises as above should be practised regularly and 'falling and rolling' training as used by volleyball players in the low dig is useful. Discussion with exponents of judo, whose early training consists of various practices on 'diffusion falling' whereby points of impact are spread out, may be of interest to prospective players and is well worth pursuing.

Because of the twisting and turning nature of the game handball players are bound to place great strain on the cartilages of the knees as well as the ligaments of the ankle. Serious injury to ligament or cartilage, of course, requires hospital treatment but the player need not be necessarily despondent as full recovery from these injuries is quite normal. Weight training to strengthen, and subsequently protect, these joints is essential.

Muscle tears in handball are common, particularly in shoulder, back and pectoral areas. For example an extended throwing arm comes through high and fast to be met with the opposition's 'rigid resistance' resulting in a tear of muscle fibre. Heat and massage can soothe the early pain and, again, rest is essential. The shoulder, like the fingers however, is a very active joint and its structure is such that it is difficult to apply supportive strappings, much more difficult than in, say, the case of calf or hamstring muscle injuries. Irrespective of site, however, reduction in activity is imperative in the case of all muscle injuries. Obviously elastic muscles are less prone to ruptures than tight ones so muscle stretching, as mentioned earlier, should be a daily part of the handball player's routine. It must always be remembered that any stretching exercises should be done slowly and gently and a sample of such exercises are listed in figures 141–145.

*Stretching pectorals* (see figure 141)

Elevate the shoulder slowly allowing the wrist to drop behind the neck. Place the elbow against a wall corner or goal post and gently push the shoulder forward against the resistance of this support.

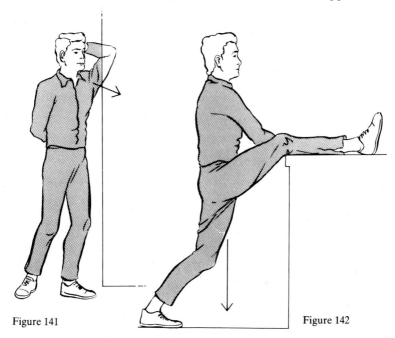

Figure 141                                                           Figure 142

*Stretching hamstrings* (see figure 142)

Place the heel bone on a table, hurdle or other solid surface. It is preferable to have a wide supporting surface coming up almost to the knee as shown. Extend the rear leg slightly backwards. To stretch the hamstrings lower the body very slowly straight downwards in the direction of the arrow as shown. Do NOT lean the chest forward towards the knee (as some people do thinking that this stretches the hamstrings – it does not!) Always have the free hand on a supporting rail or bar in case the rear leg slips during the body lowering. Again, remember, SLOWLY down till maximum is reached. Return and repeat.

*Stretching calf muscles* (see figure 143)

Lean against supporting wall as shown. Place one leg to the rear leaving only the ball of the foot in ground contact. Press the heel down till maximum stretch is felt at the back of the leg.

Figure 143

*Stretching the biceps muscle of the throwing arm*

Extend the arm backwards resting the hand on a supportive surface. Lower the body straight downwards keeping the hand in place and stretch slowly to maximum, then repeat. See figure 144.

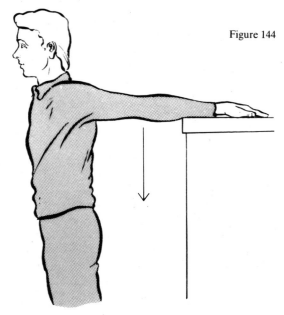

Figure 144

*Stretching Adductors*

Extend the leg to be stretched out to the side placing the hand on the outside of the thigh as shown. Now flex the other knee, pressing downwards on the thigh with the hand till the lowest point is reached. See figure 145.

Figure 145

## Cryotherapy

A comparatively new form of treatment for muscle and soft tissue injuries called cryotherapy has recently come to light. Great claims are made for its success, particularly by rugby authorities, in the healing of bruises and muscle tears in players.

Cryotherapy is the 'ice treatment' of injuries involving a mixture of cold compression and early rehabilitation movements. Traditionally the cure for muscle injuries was heat, massage and rest and whilst, in many cases, this form of treatment may still prove successful research has demonstrated that superficial heat to the skin does not penetrate deeper than approximately one-quarter of an inch below the surface. Relief was symptomatic and muscular spasm remained. Yet it is common knowledge that dilation of blood vessels brought about by heat is necessary for the repair mechanisms carried in the blood which heal torn muscle fibres. How, then, can cold treatment which, after all, is bound to *lower* body tissue temperatures affect the areas concerned? Well, in the first instance the cooling controls the bleeding of torn fibres by constricting the vessels – later, when the cold is removed, the vessels dilate with accelerated healing efficiency, a sort of compensatory, exaggerated response. (Children throwing snowballs find the snow uncomfortably cold at first but as they become warmed up their hands become redder and warmer comparatively quickly.) It is important to bandage the cold compress around the damaged area as this confines the dilation of the vessels to the deeper tissues concerned.

*Method of applying cryotherapy treatment*

The skin over the affected area should first be *carefully oiled or vaselined* prior to ice application. The ice may take the form of cubes in plastic bags or loose 'chipped' or blocked pieces as, for example, from the tray for ice cubes designed for drinks which is usually found in the deep freeze of a refrigerator. The pack is placed on the affected spot and then bandaged with towelling which has been wrung out in cold or iced water (figure 146). The bandage should be firm but not too tight. The patient, in the first instance, may complain of a stinging or burning sensation later developing into a numbness as the stinging effect diminishes; this is quite natural and

Figure 146

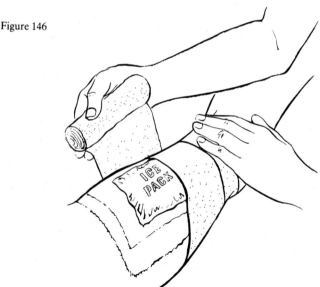

is no cause for concern. The pack should remain on the affected area for at least 20 minutes and, in the case of some of the larger muscle groups such as hamstrings and quadriceps, even longer, up to a maximum of 30 minutes (but no longer). It is even possible to massage the area using the ice pack by moving it slowly in a circular or figure-of-eight manner holding the block in a gloved hand or in a towel. On removal of the ice a large red blotch will be observed on the treated area and a firm crêpe bandage should be applied. Advise the patient to rest the limb for some hours. Early exercise should be undertaken to rehabilitate the muscle but this should be carefully graded, starting with walking, progressing to jogging and easy running long before full function is even thought of.

One or two final points worth remembering with regard to this particular form of treatment:

  (i) never apply raw ice directly to the skin – remember to oil or vaseline the skin beforehand

 (ii) the traditional heat treatment still holds fascination for many patients; there is nothing wrong with this and a combination of both ice and heat treatment can be used but *not* in the early ice treatment stages – wait till after the fifth or sixth day as superficial heat, in combination with ice soon after injury, may damage the skin and underlying tissues

(iii) do not overdo the treatment – two 30 minute applications a day are sufficient, in many instances one will suffice

 (iv) remember adequate healing time – disappearance of pain and swelling does not necessarily mean cure. Nurse that injury back to full power carefully!

  (v) muscle injuries mean that tears are replaced by scar tissue which is not as elastic as muscle fibre therefore stretching exercises to overcome this loss of elasticity should be commenced (and maintained) at the earliest possible date

# 13 Principles of refereeing

Since 1968 two referees have officiated in handball games; before that, as in soccer, only one referee controlled the match but the speed of the game was such that he could not keep up with the play nor see certain offences committed off the ball. Even with two referees it still requires a skilful and trained official to spot all the infringements which may occur.

The referees' duties begin before the game commences. They must examine the court, the goals, the ball and check that the players are correctly dressed. In addition they must ensure that players remove personal effects such as rings, bracelets, watches, etc. before going on to court. The referees are responsible for seeing that the scoresheet is accurate and that the players are numbered correctly. When going on to court they must have a watch, whistle, notebook and pen to record the score and make a note of the players guilty of misconduct.

## Dual refereeing system

Both referees time the game, record the number of goals and note the players cautioned, suspended or expelled from play. They *both* control the game and have *equal* powers of decision.

One referee is called the *goal line referee* whilst the other is the *court referee*. When a team is attacking, the goal line referee takes up a position near the goal line to one side of the goal while the court referee, as his name suggests, watches play from the centre of the court behind the attacking players slightly to the side opposite from that of his colleague. The position and movement of the referees are shown in figures 147 and 148.

The referees just simply exchange their positions according to whether a team is in defence or on the attack, thereby alternating their roles as both goal line and court referees. At half-time they remain in their respective ends of the court and do not change over. (Referee A would always control the bottom half as in the diagrams and B the top half.)

The goal line referee is responsible for infringements of the goal area, the actual taking of the penalty, corner throws, the award of goals, the movements of the goalkeeper and for fouls off the ball round the 6 metre line.

The court referee watches over play in the rear sector, in particular, shooting and tackling and is responsible for the award of free throws and penalties whilst deciding on cautions, suspensions and expulsions.

There is, of course, a certain amount of overlap in the duties of both referees and one has the authority to blow for an offence which his colleague may have missed. On occasions both might blow for

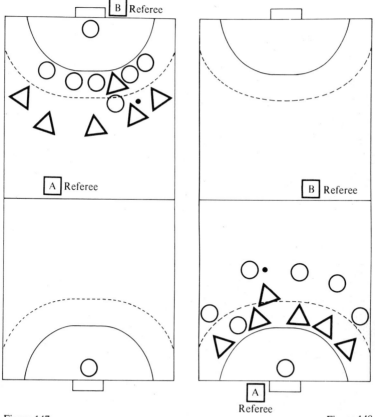

Figure 147                                                           Figure 148

Figure 149

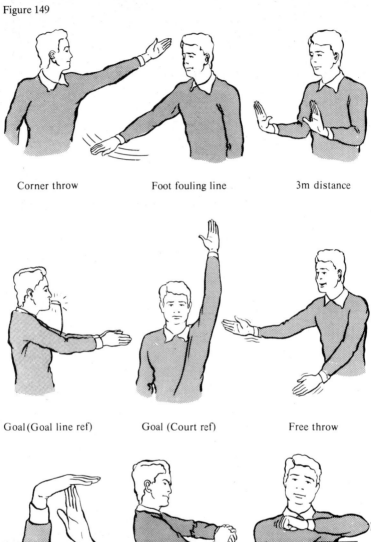

Corner throw  Foot fouling line  3m distance

Goal (Goal line ref)  Goal (Court ref)  Free throw

Time out  Time wasting  Elbowing (dangerous play)

Holding

Travelling or violating
the 3 second rule

Double dribble

Caution – yellow card

Two minute
suspension

Expulsion

Goal throw

Throw-in

Hitting

an infringement at the same time but end up by giving opposite decisions. In such cases the 'more severe' applies; the decision of the court referee overrides that of the goal line referee. If, for example, an offence is committed in confusion round the 6 metre line and the goal line referee awards a free throw to the defence and his colleague awards a free throw to the attackers, then the latter decision stands. Top-class referees with vast experience, however, avoid such contradictory situations by co-ordinating their decisions immediately an offence has been committed. Before the match the referees decide which half will be controlled by whom and at the throw-off they are in their respective positions as already described. Throughout the game only the referees have the power to enforce the laws of the game and their decisions are final. Only the team captains can appeal against their rulings.

**Referees' signals**

All players, teachers and coaches should familiarize themselves with the correct signals used by referees. They are in most instances self-explanatory (figure 149).